THE TWENTIETH CENTURY
NORFOLK

THE TWENTIETH CENTURY

NORFOLK

NEIL R. STOREY

SUTTON PUBLISHING

First published in the United Kingdom in 1999 by
Sutton Publishing Limited · Phoenix Mill
Thrupp · Stroud · Gloucestershire · GL5 2BU

British Library Cataloguing in Publication Data
A catalogue record for this book is available from the British Library.

ISBN 0-7509-2015-7

Half Title page photograph: Keep smilin' through – two little girls make the best of it during
the 1953 floods.
Title page photograph: The heart of Poppyland: 'The Garden of Sleep' at Sidestrand, *c.* 1912.

This book is dedicated to:

*My friends Basil Gowan, who encouraged the development of my writing career, and
Philip Standley, who has the dubious honour of being my father-in-law. Both of
these gentlemen have also been instrumental in making many of my books possible
by allowing me to borrow freely many images from their dilligently collected and
comprehensive archives, to draw on their knowledge, and to allow me to share their
wonderful old postcards with my readers. This book is my tribute to them, with
respectful thanks and appreciation. The way we are able to see Norfolk in the past
would not be the same without the foresight and enthusiasm of Philip and Basil.*

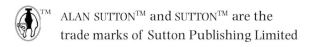
ALAN SUTTON™ and SUTTON™ are the
trade marks of Sutton Publishing Limited

Typeset in 11/14pt Photina.
Typesetting and origination by
Sutton Publishing Limited.
Printed in Great Britain by
Redwood Books, Trowbridge, Wiltshire.

Contents

Introduction   7

A New Century 1900–13   11

The First World War   35

Between the Wars   59

The Second World War   79

The Post War Years 1945–59   91

The Swinging '60s & '70s   109

Modern Times 1980–99   131

Acknowledgements   160

A Norfolk countryman and his boy, *c.* 1900.

Introduction

Norfolk has seen more dramatic and sustained change during the twentieth century than during the whole of the last millennium. With that in mind, we are indeed lucky that it was the first full century when photographers were present to record events, first on glass plate and then on film. The skilful men who made a significant contribution to capturing our Norfolk century came from many different backgrounds; some have since become well known while others remain anonymous. High standards for recording all aspects of society in the county were set during the nineteenth century by the likes of G.R. Fitt, Hugh Welch Diamond, Thomas Damant Eaton, Walter John Clutterbuck and particularly Peter Henry Emerson (1856–1936), who captured Broadland and fenland life.

Emerson was the first photographer to publish extensive portfolios of his work. Printed under simple titles like *Life and Landscape of the Norfolk Broads* (with T.F. Goodall, 1886), *Pictures of Life in Field and Fen* (1887) and *Pictures of East Anglian Life* (1888), his work quite rightly received national acclaim. Writing almost 100 years after the last of these books was published, Norwich City Librarian, Philip Hepworth, said: 'No one has more comprehensively and naturalistically photographed a human subject in action.'

With the development of the photographic picture postcard at the beginning of the twentieth century, the mantle of social documentary photography was assumed by a new generation. The leading exponent of this new medium was the popular 'social and agricultural' photographer Tom Nokes of Norwich. Heading out from his Chester Street home with camera on his bicycle's carrier and tripod strapped along the cross-bar, Tom would go on expeditions to capture images of rural life, mostly in the south of the county. Although there is no formal archive or catalogue of his work, his photographs have been avidly collected for many years.

During the 'golden age' of photographic postcards, between 1905 and 1940, certain photographers became associated with quality views of their own particular parts of Norfolk. They included Cave of Dereham, Ling of North Walsham, Tansley of Sheringham and Cromer, Yallop and Seaman of Great Yarmouth and Charles Aldous of Norwich. The most prolific of this new breed were undoubtedly the successive generations of professional photographers from the Swain family of Norwich. Their legacy is a unique archive of superb images that record city and county life in peace and war from the turn of the century to the 1970s. Indeed, some of the most famous images of the blitz in Norwich were taken by George Swain.

By the 1950s the popularity of postcards showing views or events was waning. Many local photographers and keen amateurs did struggle on until the 1970s but by then most postcard-sized images were portraits or pictures of formal groups. However, it was in the austere postwar period that a new form of social documentary photography was born – more and more images began to appear in newspapers and magazines. Names like Hallam Ashley, Ffolkes and Baldry are still remembered from this time. Nevertheless, many of the talented press photographers who had an eye for images that captured subtle changes in lifestyle and entertainment, the last days of dying crafts, and the personalities of local characters, as well as the dramatic images of disasters, rescues and storms, have been forgotten and their pictures are, sadly, unattributable.

Today there are many fine professional photographers in Norfolk. Many of them have taken images of the changing aspects of our county but only those working in the press can really record the day-to-day events now shaping life in Norfolk. That is no reason for the rest of us to be complacent, but unfortunately the likes of Tom Nokes are very rare today. In every town and village across Norfolk there will inevitably be changes: buildings, people and places will come and go; old skills may be dying out or being revived; events are still being held on greens and in parks and meadows. No matter how good or bad a photographer you think you are, why not look beyond your friends and family and dedicate a few rolls of film to recording your surroundings? Future historians will thank you for it.

A 1911 advertising card for Tom Nokes, one of the county's foremost social documentary photographers from the turn of the century. Most of his work was supplied on postcards which are still avidly collected today.

In compiling this book I am greatly indebted to those who have opened their considerable archives to me and enabled me to select images for use in these pages. The hardest decisions of all have been about what to include and what to leave out. I want not only to share these images and their captions with readers of all ages but have also striven to convey the significance of events in a Norfolk context. To do this I have recalled my own memories and mardles enjoyed with my senior compatriots while on my travels around the county or over the airwaves of BBC Radio Norfolk. To take time, sit down and think of what sticks in our minds from our own lives, and what our grandparents and great-grandparents told us about theirs, is to embark on a journey of discovery.

This book has been created by extensive trawls through archives to find previously unpublished images echoing those memories and capturing other intriguing images. It is quite amazing how one picture can bring so much to mind or lead to a new discovery after a little careful research. Examining Norfolk's history through photographs can be hard work and even frustrating at times, but it is always rewarding. New collections or single images are constantly coming to light from all manner of often unlikely sources. Frequently the most significant images arrive from people who are quite unaware of their importance – the greatest delight is to research and share the wonderful stories behind these photographs with their owners. The picture is then no longer an old piece of paper; it has become a little piece of history.

A Norfolk Century does not profess to be an authoritative account of the county in the twentieth century. Rather it is a chronological collection of memories and nostalgia to which I hope everyone can relate, regardless of whether they remember the events in question. History has created our cultural and regional identity: it is part of, and belongs to, all of us. It is up to every one of us, as its custodians, to preserve and record it for generations to come.

I hope this book will be passed down and shared with new generations in Norfolk during the new millennium so that they can see the way we were in the twentieth century. Maybe it will go some way towards inspiring them never to be ashamed of being proud of Norfolk and not to be afraid of carrying on the county tradition of 'doin' diff'rent'.

The thought I will leave you with occurred to me again and again as I researched and wrote this book, particularly when I look at the events that have taken place during my own lifetime. It is best summed up by the words of my Grandfather, George Storey, who has seen ninety years of the twentieth century and is still going strong: 'Time waits for no one and when it get a goin' bor, blas' me, that do fly!'

Keep yew orl a' troshin.

Neil R. Storey
North Walsham
November 1999

A thoughtfully composed photograph of the lane by Hockering Chapel, *c.* 1908. The consideration and skill of the local topographical photographers from the turn of the century has left us with a priceless legacy of images of Norfolk country life in the past.

A New Century
1900–13

Sir Henry Rider Haggard (1856–1925) pictured (standing, centre right) with family and friends in front of his home, Ditchingham Hall, *c.* 1908. Sir Henry left a legacy of great books including *She* and *King Solomon's Mines*. Many of his writings drew on his experiences when serving in the colonies. Not only a prolific writer, he was also a notable and radical campaigner for smallholder farming reform. An active local magistrate and public servant, he served on the Royal Commission that examined such subjects as coastal erosion, afforestation and the settlement of the poor of industrial England in the colonies, for which he received his knighthood.

Laying tram tracks, Upper King Street, Norwich, *c.* 1900. At the turn of any century thoughts of the future stimulate innovation and technological development. The introduction of a tram system to Norwich and the scale of associated area alterations was new in the experience of city residents. Whole streets were removed in the Orford Place and Castle Meadow area; this destroyed slums and created a tram centre. Once the work was completed the city had many more paved streets instead of dusty, dirty trackways and associated grime, together with a new efficient method of public transport.

One of the first trams in Norwich, the no. 38 in front of the Lord Nelson public house on Dereham Road, on its circuit to Little Orford Street, August 1900. Norwich Electric Tramways Company opened its lines for public service on 30 July 1900 with 19 miles 2 furlongs 100 yds of rail; the project had cost over £330,000 to install. The first trams ran along four routes to Magdalen Road, Earlham Road, Dereham Road and Thorpe Road. After proving to be a great success, the tram lines were rapidly extended to Unthank Road, City Road, Aylsham Road, Mousehold Heath and Trowse station.

Cromer Pier under construction, 1900. Built on the site of the old jetty, which had been severely storm damaged in 1897, the new, 500 ft pier was built by Messrs Douglass & Arnott for £18,800. It was opened with a gold key by Lord Claude Hamilton in June 1901. In 1905 a bandstand in the form of a pavilion was built at the pier head by Boulton & Paul, engineers and iron founders of Norwich. Over the next forty-five years from that acorn grew the Pavilion Theatre. Its end of the pier shows are enjoyed to this day by generations of residents and visitors alike.

In 1901 the first St John Ambulance Division in Norfolk was founded in Cromer through the efforts of local businessman Mr Robert L. Randall. It must be remembered that in those days, and indeed until 1970 in Norfolk, the only way casualties in county areas could get to hospital was by ambulances run under the auspices of the British Red Cross Society and Order of St John of Jerusalem. In those early years patients were transported in a basketwork hand-drawn litter or a horse-drawn waggon, which was in fact a coal cart fitted for stretchers. Pictured a year after formation, now fully uniformed and well trained, these are the original members of St John Ambulance, Cromer Division. Back row, left to right: C.W. Leggett, H. Needs, W.J. Darby, R. Rose, T. Smith, W. Kemp, A. Salter, B. Robson, H. Payne, F. Anderson. Front row: J. Kettle, Sgt W. Balls, Supt F.H. Barclay, Divisional Surgeon Dr A. Burton, 1st Officer F.J. Emms, Cpl J.R. Love, M. Nockels, R.L. Randall, A.J. Utting.

The Royal Arcade, Norwich's triumph of Art Deco fashion, was designed by famous city architect George Skipper. Opened in 1899, it is pictured around the time of the project's completion in 1902. The Royal Arcade was built on the site of the Royal Hotel: this had always been known as the Angel Inn, but the name was changed as a compliment to Queen Victoria on the occasion of her marriage in 1840.

Messrs F.W. Fitt and E.H. Bostock are inset to the left and right of the photograph respectively. They were the managing directors of and leading investors in the syndicate that built the Grand Opera House on St Giles Street, Norwich, in 1903. This magnificent theatre built in the Renaissance style was designed by London architect Mr W.G.R. Sprague and could seat 2,000 people. Its name was changed shortly after to The Hippodrome, and it became one of Norfolk's premier music halls and vaudeville theatres. Lloyd George spoke here, Tommy Trinder, Sandy 'Can you hear me Mother?' Powell and even Laurel and Hardy performed here. Sadly the theatre closed in 1960, and was demolished in 1966 to make way for a multi-storey car park.

One of the early annual training camps for The King's Own Royal Regiment Norfolk Imperial Yeomanry at Crown Point, Trowse, July 1904. Most of the men on parade are wearing the Other Ranks Mounted Review Order uniforms with their distinctive colonial pattern helmets and leather ammunition bandoliers, approved by King Edward VII for the raising of this regiment in 1901. Taking a personal interest in the creation of the regiment, King Edward appointed well-known and respected local officer Lt-Col Harvey Barclay of Hanworth Hall to raise it. His Majesty insisted it was designated The King's Own Royal Regiment from its inception in 1901. Such was his interest in the regiment that he helped design the dress uniforms for all ranks.

Unveiling of the South African war memorial by Maj-Gen A.S. Wynne at 2.30 pm on 17 November 1904. The memorial was erected by public subscription on Agricultural Hall Plain, Norwich, in memory of the 310 county officers and men who fell in the Boer War, 1899–1902. All Norfolk regiments and corps were represented on the monument and in the parade square. The section we can see includes the band of the Norfolk Regiment under Bandmaster Ernest Elford and the Guard of Honour provided by men from the 2nd Battalion, the Norfolk Regiment. Also present were honour guards from other Norfolk battalions, along with a squadron of 7th Dragoon Guards and a contingent from the Norfolk Yeomanry.

1905 saw a great loss to the city, with the death of one of its great civic characters – William Childerhouse, the Norwich City bellman or town crier from 1877 to 1905. In the world before radio and television criers were essential broadcasters for every city and town. Childerhouse with his stentorian voice, heralded by his expertly wielded 10 lb bell, was renowned across Norfolk. In his work proclaiming the major events in the city it is estimated that he cried 600,000 announcements and walked 70,000 miles. His corporation salary gave him 13s 4d per annum with £5 a year for civic sword-bearing and toastmastering at banquets.

The unveiling of the Sir Thomas Browne statue by Lord Avebury on 19 October 1905 at The Haymarket, Norwich. The statue, unveiled on the tercentenary of Sir Thomas's birth in 1605, commemorates one of Norfolk's greatest early writers and scholars. An accomplished physician, his analysis and defence of his profession in his book *Religio Medici* is outstanding, as is his contemplation of *Hydriotaphia or Urn Burial*.

A celebration in honour of Norfolk's greatest naval hero, Admiral Lord Nelson, was held on the centenary of his victory at the Battle of Trafalgar at the Winter Gardens, Great Yarmouth, in October 1905. Nelson was particularly dear to the people of Great Yarmouth as it was in nearby Gorleston that he set his first foot back on English soil in November 1800 after his victory at the Battle of the Nile. The great assembled crowd hailed him as the conquering hero, and the townspeople uncoupled the horses from Nelson's carriage and pulled his carriage the last leg of his journey into Great Yarmouth market-place for his official reception, at which he received the freedom of the borough. A reconstruction of this magnificent event is planned for November 2000.

Hunstanton's lifeboat *Licensed Victualler* is pulled through the streets of King's Lynn on its launch carriage on Foresters Gala. The boat is pulled by the horses which would trot into the sea to launch it. From the 1890s until the beginning of the First World War lifeboats would be seen on parade in their locality at least once a year on Lifeboat Saturday to raise awareness and money for the RNLI. In 1915 Lifeboat Flag Day was introduced as its main annual fund-raising event.

Emigrants gather for one last photograph before leaving for Canada from Norwich on Wednesday 6 March 1907. The group includes families with children as young as eleven months. All of those seen here were sent out through the agency of the Norwich Distress Committee. All of their hopes must have been high; posters, publicity and sponsorship called for unskilled labourers, navvies, domestic servants and all willing workers to go to 'Britains nearest and greatest colony'. Tennant farmers were tempted by offers of 160 acres free in the country that offered 'Happy homes, healthy bracing climate, cheap fares and comfortable speedy travel'.

The grand procession on the opening day of the Church Congress held at Great Yarmouth on Tuesday 1 October 1907. The thoroughfares along the route were crammed with spectators and shops closed temporarily as the grand procession passed. The photograph shows the section led by the Great Yarmouth Mace, Oar and Sword Bearers, followed by the Recorder, the Mayor, High Steward, Lord Lieutenant of Norfolk and the High Sheriff of Norwich. Behind them are the lay members of the congress, Parochial Clergy, rural deans, canons and archdeacons. The congress included speeches on topics as diverse as socialism, Dr Barnardo's Orphans Homes with a display from the boys at Watt's Naval Training College and the church and the herring industry. The congress concluded on Friday 4 October 1907.

Tombland Fair, Norwich, 1907. The festivities are recorded as far back as the twelfth century and probably have their origin in even earlier celebrations. The fair takes its name from Tombland (a corruption of the Saxon word meaning open space), where the fair was held for over 600 years. In 1818, when complaints made by residents about the prolonged noise and disruption caused by the event were upheld in court, the fair was ordered to move. It found a new home on a site beside the Agricultural Hall and across the cattle market. When most of this area was developed for Castle Mall in the 1990s the fair was moved on to Castle Meadow.

Proclamation of Lynn Mart, 1908. After the attractions and rides have been wintered, repaired and repainted in the town, Lynn Mart is held as the traditional beginning of the annual Norfolk fair circuit. The Mart always begins on 14 February (no connection with St Valentine's Day) and is traditionally opened by the Mayor of King's Lynn accompanied by complete civic entourage.

The Cock Inn, Lakenham, is seen burnt out on 31 March 1908. High winds fanning the fire that had engulfed the nearby Lakenham Mill blew sparks that caught on the dry old thatched roof of the pub and an adjacent house. It was not long before these buildings were also engulfed in flames. Both were rebuilt shortly after and the pub is still serving today.

The May King and Queen with maids of honour and members of their procession pose for this group photograph with their teachers during The Norwich Grand Floral Festival held on 20, 21 and 23 May 1908 at St Andrew's Hall. Organised by The Norwich and Norfolk Gospel Temperance Band of Hope Union over 600 children took part. They entertained audiences with part songs by a united choir, 'popular and up to date action songs' culminating with the crowning of the May Queen.

The first ever training camp of the 6th (Cyclist) Battalion, the Norfolk Regiment (TF) at Northrepps Hall, 1908. Richard Burdon Haldane, the new Liberal government's War Secretary, had the duty of implementing the Esher Report. This completely reformed the British Army and created a territorial force instead of the old volunteer system. This new scheme included provision for a number of British regiments to have territorial cyclist battalions. Norfolk was selected as one of them, and under the energetic command of Lt-Col Bernard Henry Leathes Prior the 6th Battalion (Cyclists) of the Norfolk Regiment was raised, initially with 4 officers and 176 men selected from all the old volunteer battalions.

A crowd gathers in front of the Maid's Head Inn on Spixworth Road, Old Catton, 2 November 1908. They are awaiting the result of the inquest into the death of nineteen-year-old Nellie Howard whose body was found nearby. The verdict returned was wilful murder. Her suitor, Horace Larter, was apprehended, brought to trial and convicted. He was executed at Norwich Gaol for the crime.

Thetford 1st XI football team for the season 1909/10. Formed in 1883, in their early years they were affiliated to Suffolk Football Association and were Suffolk Junior Cup winners in 1911. They won the Norfolk Senior Cup in 1948 and Norfolk Senior Amateur Cup in 1955. Norfolk has a long tradition of keenly played and supported village and town football. A series of leagues and cup championships have been successively formed. The oldest, which is still competed for, is the Norfolk County Football Association Senior Cup, founded the same year as the Association in 1881.

King Edward VII on his last visit to Norwich, Monday 25 October 1909. On a full and active visit His Majesty laid the foundation stone for the extension at the Norfolk and Norwich Hospital, gave an address at St Andrew's Hall and had luncheon with the officers at the Chapel Field Drill Hall. In the afternoon he proceeded to Mousehold Heath to be greeted by 11,000 schoolchildren on the mound. The King then presented new colours to and reviewed the 3,000-strong Territorial Force and parade of veterans from the Royal Norfolk Veterans Association.

Suffragette rally around the statue of the Duke of Wellington, Norwich Market Place, *c.* 1909. At this time the votes for women movement was growing in momentum. In London there had been some of the largest demonstrations the capital had ever seen but still the women were no closer to attaining their goals, so it was decided that more drastic action should be employed to raise awareness of their cause. In London pictures at the National Gallery were slashed and plants were destroyed at Kew. In Norfolk suffragettes crept into public meetings, church and even cathedral services, shouting out slogans at pre-arranged moments, and holding up 'Votes for Women' placards.

The suffragette campaign adopted ever more drastic and dangerous means of protest. They threatened to explode bombs across the country. The latest tactic in 1909 was women deliberately seeking terms of imprisonment. This was often done by publicly smashing shop windows. There were a number of such instances across Norfolk. The worst of all the protests was probably not intended to go as far as it did: suffragettes started a fire in the Pavilion Theatre on Britannia Pier, Great Yarmouth on 22 December 1909. Fanned by high winds, the fire spread rapidly through the wood and iron structure: if you look closely at the photograph you will see members of the public watching the fire from very close quarters – rather them than me!

A display by members of the 16th Lancers at the Cavalry Barracks, Barrack Street, Norwich, 10 February 1911. This was a popular venue for military spectacles and entertainment since it opened in 1791; hundreds would gather round the parade square for Sunday music performances. Children would gather at the gates on Sunday mornings to follow parades of mounted troops on their way to a service at Norwich Cathedral. Later known as Nelson Barracks, it served Norfolk soldiers faithfully through two world wars, but was sadly dilapidated by 1965 when it was demolished. The site was landscaped and used as building land for council housing.

Crowds throng Norwich Market Place in front of the old municipal buildings to hear Dr E.E. Blyth, the first Lord Mayor of Norwich, read the formal proclamation of the accession of HM King George V on 9 May 1910. The square surrounding the platform is lined by members of the 16th Lancers, the Norfolk Regiment and the King's Own Royal Regiment Norfolk Yeomanry.

Coronation Day was 22 June 1911, and across the country festivities were preceded by church services. Leading the religious events in Norfolk was the great service in Norwich Cathedral, led by the Bishop, the Right Revd Bertram Pollock DD, CVO. Seen here shortly after its close, civil dignitaries and city officials process out with due pomp and ceremony.

Celebrations for the coronation of George V were held in every town and village across Norfolk on Thursday 22 June 1911. After short ceremonies of flag raising and bands playing, most places began their main celebrations with a united service. Here we see some of the festivities in Wymondham Market Place. Coronation luncheons and teas were shared by townspeople, often in the open air, and every child received a coronation mug. To complete the entertainments coronation sports for all ages were held on nearby meadows, greens or parkland in the afternoon.

Schoolchildren, under the direction of a master with an ominously big stick, rehearse their singing for the visit of King George V at Thorpe Hamlet School, June 1911.

HM King George V in his carriage, complete with mounted escort provided by members of the King's Own Royal Regiment, Norfolk Yeomanry, during his first visit to Norwich as King on 28 June 1911. He is seen here in Norwich Market Place in front of the old municipal buildings, where thousands of children were crammed to 'sing the King in'.

Bentfield C. Hucks, acknowledged as the first man to fly over Norwich. This momentous occasion happened on 10 August 1912. Hucks flew a Blériot monoplane, tail number 16, named 'Firefly' from Crow Hall Farm, Gorleston, to Church Lane, Eaton. The *Eastern Daily Press* recorded the event: 'The first sighting of the monoplane sent a thrill of excitement through the crowd. It appeared but a dark speck moving almost imperceptibly through the vast spaces of the horizon.' Once he was over the landing ground there were wild cheers of 'Bravo Hucks'. He was feted when he landed and many women wanted autographs, but he politely declined. On his flight from Great Yarmouth to Acle Hucks followed the main road, and afterwards the railway line. Because of a thick brown mist he only picked up Norwich because the river with the sun shining on it 'looked like molten gold'.

One of the rescue boats with its oarsman and police officer stands by to help evacuate one of the collapsed houses on Lothian Street, Monday 26 August 1912. On this day Norwich saw its worst flood of the twentieth century. It had been a wet season: in the opening weeks of August over 11 inches, about half an annual average rainfall, was recorded in Norwich. The whole county was saturated and with 7.5 inches of rainfall in forty-eight hours over Norwich. Water fell on the higher ground to the west and north of the city, and the River Wensum burst and swept over its banks to rush along the streets, becoming a deadly and destructive fast-flowing river through the city.

Despite being about 1 ft deep in water and having been subject to the worst flood in living memory, they were still serving (and still had customers to serve) at the Causeway Tavern on the corner of Russell Street, Norwich, 26 August 1912.

Magdalen Street. By 28 August 1912 the waters had subsided, but with some streets up to 10 ft deep in water it took a long time to drain away. As seen here, carts were not only used to evacuate and rescue people and possessions from houses, but also took visitors on tours of the worst affected areas for 1*d* a time. Carts also took round special deliveries of basic groceries, fuel and candles throughout the following days. Deliveries were even made from the roof of waggons to those who had decided to stay in the upper storeys of their houses.

After the flood at Loddon Mill, 28 August 1912. Not only Norwich was affected by the flood of 26 August. Many rural areas were stranded as quiet rivers swelled to raging forces of water which swept away bridges, fracturing roadways and carrying railway lines into the foaming waters. Thousands of acres of farmland were awash and most of the ripe harvest was ruined, causing yet more hardship for rural communities in the wake of the flood.

Some of the 6,000 applicants, supervised by local police, lining up in front of St Andrew's Hall to claim relief for flood damage, 28 August 1912. Damage across the county amounted to over £100,000, with 15,000 people losing homes or property.

Clearing up the granite and wooden pavements destroyed on Duke Street, Norwich, August 1912. This sight was a familiar one across the city. As the waters receded or were pumped away, debris and collapsed buildings had to be cleared. The clean-up and repair operation was massive. In the city alone over 750 acres and 3,650 buildings, including 33 churches and 59 factories, had been affected.

Sea Cadets and Cadet Norfolk Artillery on parade aboard the training ship *Lord Nelson*, near Bishop Bridge, Norwich. The Norwich Sea Cadet Corps is the oldest in Norfolk. It was first proposed by the Norfolk and Norwich Navy League in 1911. By February 1912, after a well-attended public meeting in the Guildhall, £500 had been subscribed for the purchase of a vessel and annual subscriptions amounting to £30 to meet maintenance and running costs. With this money the Lowestoft sailing trawler *Elsie* was fitted out as a training brig, re-christened *Lord Nelson*, and was dedicated that boys 'might be trained in the rudiments of seamanship and acquire a taste for ocean life' on 24 June 1912. *Lord Nelson* served the Sea Cadets faithfully until 1938 when it was replaced by a newer boat.

The day the 'Red Army' invaded: members of the Coldstream Guards move out from Swaffham Market Place, 1912. Throughout most of the summer of 1912 one of the largest military exercises ever carried out in Norfolk was enacted throughout Breckland. Centred on the towns of Thetford and Swaffham, all manner of troops could be found – ranging from the Grenadier and Coldstream Guards to cavalry and even the Royal Engineers' Balloon Observation Section. The 'red' army had invaded and the 'yellow' army was defending.

Boys from Norwich companies of the Boys' Brigade happy in their work on washing up duty at their annual camp at Mundesley, 1913.

Sexton's Shoe Factory, Fishergate, Norwich, was destroyed by fire on 16 January 1913. Following an earlier fire in 1900 Sexton's had set up their own fire brigade. With the absence of an effective Norwich City Fire Brigade, other companies and organisations like Colmans, Boulton & Paul, Steward & Patteson and the military at Britannia Barracks had had their own fire brigades for many years to attend incidents at their works or fires in areas near to their respective localities. Sadly in this instance the fire broke out in the early hours of the morning when the factory was closed, so the Sexton's brigade could not get to its appliance before the blaze blocked the entrance. Caley's Works Brigade was called, but by the time it arrived all it could do was quell the fire that had burnt the factory to a shell.

Norwich Horse Fair, Prince of Wales Road, 1913. At the turn of the century, when just about every business – whether itinerant trader, hawker or shop with a delivery round – had a horse and cart, often beautifully painted, the carts brightened up the highways and byways as they trotted by. This is probably the last Norwich Horse Parade, when all the roundsmen and drivers would ensure the carts were cleaned and repainted and the horses groomed with their tails and manes trimmed and braided, and all horse brasses given an even more thorough polish. This grand prade was never to be repeated after the First World War, because of increasing automation.

At 2.15 pm precisely on Monday 27 April 1914 Miss Olga Mills steps out from her parent's house, 'Fairfield' on Lime Tree Road, Norwich, resplendent in her bridal gown of ivory crepe meteor satin. She is accompanied by her father, influential Norwich solicitor Henry Jacob Mills. The car awaits to drive them to Christ Church, Eaton, where she was to marry Mr John P. Tilley. Anybody who was anybody in the Norfolk social set was there. The guest list reads like a Norfolk who's who and the present list like a catalogue from Fortnum & Mason's. This event was crowned by a sumptuous garden party at 'Fairfield', where refreshments were served by Mrs Pillow of Prince's Restaurant.

Queen Alexandra Day at Norwich, 24 June 1914. A hospital-based charity, Queen Alexandra Day focused that year on raising funds for the Jenny Lind Hospital for Sick Children.

Burston School, 1914. This photograph is typical of hundreds of school groups taken across the county in the early years of the twentieth century. The events that happened at this school in the months after this photogrpah was taken make it unique, however. The schoolmaster and schoolmistress are Tom and Kitty Higdon who took up teaching posts here in 1911. They were soon recognised as enthusiastic and talented teachers, generous and fair to their pupils; they quickly became accepted as well-liked members of the local community. Times were hard in the country then but the Higdons wanted to improve conditions and resources at the school. Tom also became involved in trade union activities. All of this met with fierce opposition from the rector, the Revd Charles Tucker Eland, who was also chairman of the school governors. The friction resulted in a bizarre series of events, culminating with a dismissal notice being presented to the Higdons on 29 March 1914 – which gave them two days' notice. One of the school's first-class students, Violet Potter, had collected a list of names of children willing to go on strike in protest at this, and on 1 April they did. A rival school, where the Higdons were employed, was built by public subscription in 1917 but the dispute went on, involving national trade union and socialist campaigners, until it was resolved in the Higdons' favour shortly before the Second World War.

The First World War

Men of the Norfolk and Suffolk Territorial Brigade (about 2,000 strong) under Col R. Bayard
DSO march past the Earl of Leicester, Lord Lieutenant of Norfolk, at Holkham Park, July 1914.
This was the last review of the local Territorials before the outbreak of the war on
4 August 1914. Many of these men returned home to find mobilisation papers (sent out on
29 July) waiting for them, and they would not be 'out of uniform' for the duration.

Mobilisation at King's Lynn station, 5 August 1914. With cheers and cheerios the boys of A Company, 5th Battalion, the Norfolk Regiment, leave King's Lynn station to muster with their comrades from other companies at their headquarters in East Dereham. These were territorial soldiers, leaving their homes and jobs to fight on some foreign field. None of them could have possibly imagined that they would be sent to Turkey to fight in the Gallipoli Peninsula. The casualties received by the 4th and 5th Battalions were horrific. If bullets did not get them, infections and disease could. Very few of the men who left on this happy day returned to see their beloved county again.

Men of the 4th Battalion preparing to leave the Midland and Great Northern Railway city station, August 1914.

The XII (Prince of Wales's Royal) Lancers, who had been stationed at the Cavalry Barracks since 1912, mobilised for war from there in August 1914. Preparations to take the unit over to France were rapidly made, and the men are seen here with their Commanding Officer Lt-Col F. Wormold making ready to depart on the first leg of their journey to France from Thorpe station, Norwich, on 16 August 1914.

Volunteers for Kitchener's Army on the march down Bank Plain, Norwich, August 1914. When war broke out it was widely believed that the conflict would all be over by Christmas. Lord Kitchener was one of the few senior officials who would admit this was not the case, and that we would need more than the 235,000 'first line' regular army troops (half of whom were on foreign service) to fight. On 11 August 1914 the famous 'Your King and Country Need You!' poster with the imposing face and inescapable finger of Kitchener was published. It called for 'K1', his first 100,000 men aged between nineteen and thirty, to enlist. Once the piecemeal uniforms had been issued and basic local training completed, most of these men would be sent to Shorncliffe Camp. Once on active service many would find themselves part of the 12th and 18th Divisions on the Western Front

About 4,000 men of the 2nd Battalion Essex Regiment cram into Norwich Market Place, 10 August 1914.

On 10 August 1914 enterprising city barbers saw that many of these men from the Essex Regiment were recent recruits, who had worked hard on training and building up their kit but whose personal appearance needed a bit of a smarten up. They brought their chairs out from their shops and under the watchful eye of the sergeants provide shaves and military haircuts for the soldiers.

Settled in at their camp, men of the 1/4th Battalion Essex Regiment, complete with their band, parade down St Augustine's Street, August 1914.

New recruits for the 4th (Territorial) Battalion marching down Earlham Road, 1914. It is said that every time they marched out they would come back with more than they left with; a few more men would join on the back of the parade and volunteer. About 700 men were recruited from south and east Norfolk, and in Norwich about 700 men were recruited in the first four weeks of the outbreak of war. So many volunteered that a 2/4th was created to help administration. Barracking men in the city, however, was impossible, so they were billetted in private houses with subsistence. The householders were paid 2s 6d a day.

Men of the 1st East Anglian Brigade, Royal Field Artillery enjoy a musical interlude at the end of a hard day's troshin' in the fields, 1914. War or no war, there was still a harvest to get in. Many of the young men who normally helped with the harvest had joined up and gone away to war. Where difficulties in harvesting were encountered it was not unknown for soldiers to be dispatched to lend a hand.

The brave, smiling faces of August 1914 turn to looks of concern and suffering as casualties, having filled the London hospitals, are sent out to the provinces. This photograph shows one of the first wounded soldiers being unloaded from the first trainload of casualties brought to Norwich on 17 October 1914. From the first day there were often crowds of mothers, wives and sweethearts waiting at the gates of the station for the hospital transport convoys to pass through. They would throw flowers into the backs of the passing ambulances.

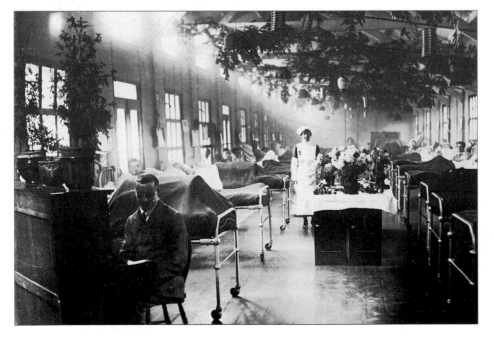

A ward of wounded soldiers at the Norfolk and Norwich Hospital, December 1914. The Christmas decorations are up and there are still a few smiles on the faces of these men wounded in the opening battles of the First World War. At the piano is Billy Howard, who was blinded during the Battle of Mons. He did not lose his skill with the keys and he played in the various hospital wards to entertain his wounded comrades.

The first parade of the City of Norwich Volunteers (Volunteer Training Corps), 15 December 1914. With the fear of attack or even invasion in many people's minds, home defence was 'A consideration for every able bodied man, who for whatever reason, is not currently serving with the colours': so read a leaflet that circulated early in the war, when men who were too old or unsuitable to serve in the forces were encouraged to join a Volunteer Training Corps – in effect a First World War equivalent of the Home Guard.

A parade of the Norwich Civilians Emergency Corps, December 1915. Each man wears the only item of insignia worn by the Corps, the lapel badge; each was produced in a white metal in the form of an ornate shield bearing the arms of Norwich with the members' personal number embossed underneath. The Corps worked as a kind of civil defence unit, which would work to clear wrecked houses, recover casualties and repair damage 'if spies sabotaged utilities or vital lines of transport'.

The first bomb ever dropped in anger on a civilian target from an aircraft fell on Whitehall Yard, Wymondham Street, Sheringham, at about 8.30 pm on Tuesday 19 January 1915. It smashed through the roof and came to rest a few feet away from a baby's crib. Luckily it did not go off. This attack was devised by Admiral von Pohl, Chief of the Imperial German Naval Staff, and the Kaiser himself. The attack was led by Fregattenkapitän Peter Strasser, Chief of the German Naval Airship Division. Three airships, the L3, L4 and L6 (under Strasser), took off for the mission from Nordholz. However, the L6 developed engine trouble and had to turn back, much to the disgust of Strasser. The L4 made landfall over Bacton: her commander, Kapitänleutnant Magnus Count von Platen Hallermand, thought he was over the Humber and dropped a couple of bombs on Sheringham.

The scene at St Peter's Plain after Great Yarmouth was bombed on 19 January 1915. Zeppelin L3 under the command of Kapitänleutnant Hans Fritz made landfall a short distance from L4 at Happisburgh, and skirted the coastline towards Great Yarmouth. Here he turned landwards and dropped a series of high explosive and incendiary bombs on the Drakes Building/St Peter's Plain area, where the first fatalities of the raid took place: Mrs Martha Taylor and Samuel Smith the shoemaker. Dropping a few more bombs as it flew over the fish wharf, the Zeppelin turned seaward. A patrol of the 1/6th (Cyclist) Battalion, the Norfolk Regiment, opened fire, causing superficial damage to the Zeppelin.

Zeppelin L4, having bombed Sheringham, followed the coastline and was spotted over Weybourne and Holt. His next bomb was dropped on Heacham but it did not explode. An armed guard from the locally stationed Derbeyshire Yeomanry was put on the device and was joined by the local bobby to ensure the interested crowd did not get too curious.

Workmen pause for the photographer while cutting boards to cover the damaged windows of St Mary's Church, Snettisham, on 20 January 1915. After Heacham, the next bomb dropped by L4 on the raid of 19 January 1915 was a heavy explosive launched on Snettisham, which did explode and blasted out the great east window over the chancel and two other windows behind the organ. The east window was replaced by an inset stained-glass window as a memorial to the men from the village who fell in the First World War.

The houses on Bentinck Street, King's Lynn, where Mrs Maude Gazley (whose husband had recently been killed on the Western Front) and fifteen-year-old Percy Goate lived: they were to be the last fatal casualties in the raid of 19 January 1915. The bombs were dropped from Zeppelin L4. Its commander Kapitänleutnant Magnus Count von Platen Hallermand was ignorant of his position, and believing that he was attacking 'fortified places between the Tyne and Humber' he circled King's Lynn twice and dropped his seven remaining bombs over the town, killing two and injuring thirteen.

Piled into their insurance agent's car is one of the King's Lynn families whose houses were wrecked by the high explosive bombs dropped on the town during the Zeppelin raid of 19 January 1915. They are being seen off by sympathetic neighbours, many of whom did not have the luxury of insurance.

Pictured when newly commissioned in 1915, this is the late CSM Harry Daniels, 2nd Battalion, The Rifle Brigade. He was Norfolk's first recipient, during the First World War, of the the Victoria Cross, our nation's highest gallantry award. He was born in Wymondham in 1884 and both his parents died when he was still a young lad. Put in the Norwich Boys' Home on Faiths Lane, he ran away to join The Rifle Brigade as a boy soldier. By 12 March 1915 he was a Company Sergeant Major. During the battle of Neuve Chappelle, France, he could see his battalion's advance, due for the following morning, would be impeded by wire entanglements. CSM Daniels and Cpl 'Tom' Noble voluntarily went over the top under severe machine-gun fire armed only with wire cutters. Both were wounded almost immediately but they kept cutting until their job was done when 'Tom' took a fatal bullet in the chest. Harry, although badly wounded, managed to crawl back. For their gallant actions they were both awarded the Victoria Cross. Harry returned to a befitting hero's welcome in Norfolk where, after official greetings, he visited his old boys home. 'Dan VC' was commissioned a few weeks later and he went on to be decorated again with the MC for another brave action. After a distinguished military career he retired as a Lieutenant-Colonel in 1942 and joined 'civvy street' as manager of the Leeds Opera House. He died in Leeds on 13 December 1953, his last request being that his ashes should be scattered on Aldershot cricket pitch.

One of the Royal Army Medical Corps Ambulance Trains halts on St Augustine's in Norwich, *c.* 1915. Jugs of water are brought out for the convalescent casualties, who were being carried to Voluntary Aid Detachment (VAD) hospitals across Norfolk.

Interior of the annexe canteen at The Norfolk War Hospital, *c.* 1915. As casualties were sent up to Norfolk with horrifying regularity the Norfolk and Norwich Hospital was stretched to the limit. A new extension ward was funded by subscriptions from readers of the *Eastern Daily Press* in February 1915 and emergency shed wards were built in the grounds of the hospital. In 1914 the need was such that the asylum at Thorpe had its patients transferred; the hospital was then occupied by returned wounded service personnel and became known as The Norfolk War Hospital.

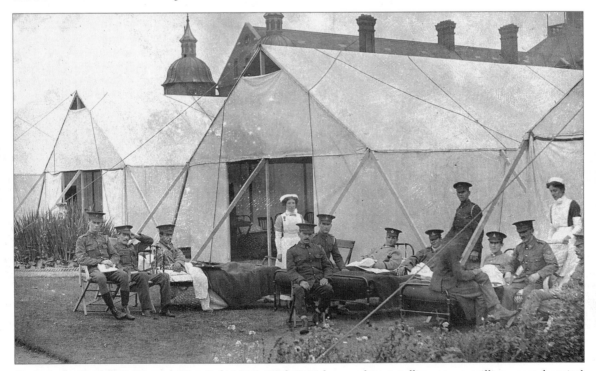

Tent wards, Norfolk & Norwich Hospital, 1915. With British casualties totalling over a million every hospital bed was needed. All available floorspace was eventually used up so drastic measures had to be taken. Tents were erected in the grounds for recuperating soldiers.

Members of the Lincolnshire Yeomanry on the range at Garboldisham, *c.* 1915. It seemed as if all of England's fields and parks became encampments for troops in training or transit. Once units were embodied or raised the soldiers would find they were soon sent to other areas of the country, the thinking being that men should be taken away from their home area to concentrate on working and living together as soldiers, rather than getting home at the end of the day or every weekend.

Men from A&B Squadrons of the Middlesex Hussars after digging their trench lines at Blickling, 1915. The diversity of units that passed through Norfolk during the First World War was truly amazing. At Aylsham alone men from the Royal Army Medical Corps, the Pembroke Yeomanry, the Glamorgan Yeomanry, the 3rd City of London Yeomanry ('The Sharpshooters'), and the Rough Riders were all stationed in or around the town in the early years of the First World War.

The pipes of the Black Watch on parade in Norwich Cathedral Close, *c.* 1915. Despite there being a wide variety of troops passing through Norwich and Norfolk, probably none caused such a stir and spectacle as the men from Scottish regiments resplendent in their bright Glengarrys, smart cut-away tunics, kilts, spats and sporrans. I don't think local people had ever seen or heard anything quite like it.

Some of the wrecked shops and houses on Church Street, East Dereham, after the first Zeppelin raid in the town on 9 September 1915. As the war progressed Zeppelins began to penetrate deeper into England and even drop bombs on London. The first raid of this kind was undertaken by Zeppelin L3 on 8 September 1915 when bombs were dropped in a line from Euston to Liverpool Street, killing twenty-six people. It was during this same raid that bombs were dropped on East Dereham, causing extensive damage to the town and killing Harry Patterson, a watchmaker and jeweller, James Taylor, a general dealer, and Lance-Cpl Alfred Pomeroy of the 2/1st City of London Yeomanry. There were also a number of people who suffered injuries in the attack, two of whom later died of their wounds.

Men from HQ Company Cycling School, 1/6th (Cyclist) Battalion, the Norfolk Regiment, North Walsham, 10 September 1915. Most of those pictured are wearing shorts, the form of dress adopted for all cyclist troops in summer months when in training or on manoeuvres. Recruit cyclists would wear shorts until they were proved competent riders, whatever the season. This was done to avoid them constantly tearing the knees out of their service dress trousers when they fell off their bikes. With the threat of invasion and attack from Zeppelins, coastal defence was enacted under the Home Defence Scheme, whereby the observation and patrol defences of the British coast were entrusted to certain mounted and cycle corps of the Territorial Army. In Norfolk this task was the responsibility of the 1/6th (Cyclist) Battalion, the Norfolk Regiment, under Col Bernard Henry Leathes Prior DSO, TD. Its headquarters was at Park Hall, North Walsham, with detachments stationed along the coastal patrol area from Wells to Gorleston.

Street collectors ready to go out into Gorleston to sell pin 'flags' for 'Our Day', 21 October 1915. The collection was used to help fund the hospitals, ambulance transports, aid and comforts supplied by the Joint Council of the British Red Cross Society and the Order of St John of Jerusalem.

A detachment of the Royal Navy Anti-Aircraft Mobile Brigade at North Walsham, April 1916. 'Super-Zeppelins' were being developed to raid London and more assertive measures were needed to combat the menace. This detachment was sent to Norfolk as part of the first line defences of London because the nearby Happisburgh lightship was used as a guide beacon for Zeppelin raiders on their way to the capital. There were many frustrated exchanges between the Anti-Aircraft Brigade maintaining their vigil on the Happisburgh cliff-top and the captain of the Happisburgh lightship when they requested that he turn his light off!

Patients and nurses from Woodbastwick Hall VAD Hospital, *c.* 1917. As the hospitals were being stretched to breaking point in Norwich by the constant arrival of returned wounded, an appeal was put out from the Joint War Committee of the British Red Cross Society and the Order of St John of Jerusalem across Norfolk for people with sizeable properties to consider allowing at least part of them to be used as auxiliary war hospitals for convalescent servicemen. The first to receive casualties was Woodbastwick Hall, on 28 September 1914. The Hall, under its Commandant Mrs Maude Cator, provided 100 beds and even had an operating theatre. When it closed on 19 December 1918 it had admitted 1,113 patients.

Members of the 1st (City of Norwich) Battalion, Norfolk Volunteers being inspected by Colonel, the Earl of Leicester GCVO, CM, ADC, Regimental Commandant, accompanied by Lt-Col Leathes Prior VD, 26 September 1915. They had come a long way since 1914; with training from Regular Army instructors, and issued with uniforms and rifles, they looked a smart and proud body of men.

Men of the Norwich Volunteers having a break while on exercise on the outskirts of the city, c. 1916. They trained at weekends, like territorial soldiers, in battle skills and drill. They undertook a wide variety of duties, ranging from providing armed guards on bridges, utility stations and transport centres, to helping guide the airships into the hangars at Pulham Air Station.

A massed parade of all battalions of the City of Norwich Volunteers and representatives from the Norfolk Volunteers in front of Norwich Cathedral, c. 1916. These men 'did their bit' in their own way throughout the First World War. It was often a thankless task; though the average age of the volunteers was forty-four and cruel nicknames were attached to them, such as 'The Cripples Brigade' and 'England's Last Hope'.

Crashed Sopwith Pup, Black Dyke, Feltwell, *c.* 1917. Feltwell airfield, with a grass runway, was opened in November 1917 as the base of No. 7 Training Depot Station, Royal Flying Corps. Many types of aircraft flew out of this station including SE.5s, DH4s, Avro 504s and Sopwith Pups. Because this was a training station sadly flying accidents were not uncommon and trucks carrying medics and mechanics would often be seen speeding along the lanes to recover pilots and their smashed aircraft. In those days pilots had no option of baling out: parachutes had not been developed by 1917.

Members of Loddon British Red Cross Society and convalescent troops from Loddon VAD Hospital gather for the camera on the occasion of the 'Our Day' collection, Monday 15 October 1917. Behind the poster in the centre of the group is the hospital Commandant Mrs McClintock. The VAD hospital was opened on 19 November 1914 and was situated in the lecture hall of the Methodist chapel where there were twenty beds available. On 2 October 1918 the premises were destroyed by fire, but six days later the Revd J. Mattinson offered the vicarage, and by 26 October it was operational. The hospitals here treated 474 patients and closed on 23 November 1918. Overall, Norfolk provided 62 VAD hospitals between 1914 and 1919, and admitted a total of 35,736 convalescent soldiers looked after by 3,132 voluntary nurses.

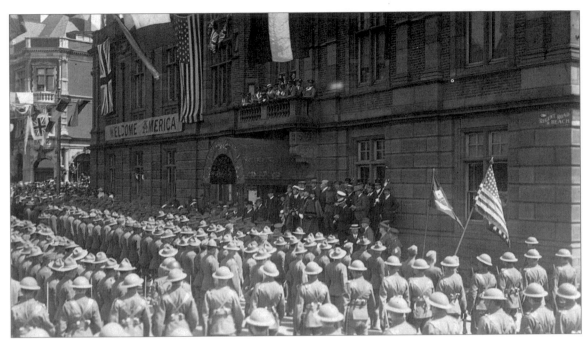

Great Yarmouth welcomes America, 4 July 1918. Over 500 American troops arrived at Vauxhall station from where they marched down North Quay to the official reception seen here in front of Great Yarmouth Town Hall. Afterwards a baseball match was played at the Wellesley Recreation Ground, and the day was completed by a dance at the recreation rooms.

Maj Egbert Cadbury, brother officers and senior ratings join the members of the Royal Naval Air Service football team who won the Yarmouth Services League shield 1917/18 season. Based on the South Denes at Great Yarmouth, flying Sopwith seaplanes, the unit flew operational sorties to monitor enemy shipping and to engage enemy aircraft and airships. The final active sortie of the war was flown from the station on 5 August 1918 when Maj Cadbury shot down Zeppelin L70.

The Wing Boys Concert Party, No. 2 Coastal Airship Station, Pulham St Mary, early 1918. As the airship station became established more men were stationed there, including an RFC unit of skilled engineers, electricians, bricklayers and joiners – the Air Construction Service – and RAF Parachute Experimental Staff. Greater efforts at evening entertainments and performances were made, and inevitably this variety concert party was formed.

Mr T.E. Byron speaks from the top of the tank on Labour Day, part of Tank Week, Norwich, Monday 1 to Saturday 6 April 1918. The week, a drive to raise money for the war effort with members of the public purchasing war bonds in the Guildhall, raised £1,057,382 in Norwich alone.

One almighty cheer goes up from the officers and men of the 51st and 52nd (Graduated) Battalion, The Bedfordshire Regiment in Norwich Market Place on the eleventh hour of the eleventh day of the eleventh month 1918. It was Armistice Day and the end of the First World War.

Wymondham Gun Week, Tuesday 12 November 1918. Planned well before the announcement of the Armistice the previous day, the Gun Week went ahead. The gun, which had seen action in France, was drawn into Wymondham Market Place by a team of mules from the station. The parade, led by a band from the Norfolk Regiment, also included soldiers well enough to march from the local VAD hospital. Silver War Badge-wearing discharged soldiers, special constables and a host of local civilian organisations finished up at the market cross, where speeches were given. After just the first day £7,088 had been raised for the war effort.

The Colours of the Norfolk Regiment lead the parade up Upper King Street from the cathedral for Norwich's Peace Day Parade, 19 July 1919. When the Armistice was declared there were great celebrations, but they were not complete because the boys (and girls) weren't back. With Norfolk men and women in theatres of war as far apart as France and Salonika, Germany, Palestine and Egypt it was going to take quite some time for many of them to come home. Across the country a summer date of 19 July 1919 was set for the united Peace Day celebrations.

Norfolk's greatest heroine. Nurse Edith Cavell was born in 1865. She was the daughter of the Vicar of Swardeston and from her earliest years she dedicated herself to caring for others. Working from her clinic in Brussels she treated both British and German casualties. Nurse Cavell became part of an underground escape network for Allied soldiers but was betrayed and condemned to death under the charge of 'conducting soldiers to the enemy'. Taken to a firing range, she was executed on 12 October 1915.

A crowd of thousands crammed into Tombland, Norwich, to witness the unveiling of the memorial to Nurse Edith Cavell, patriot and martyr, on 12 October 1918 – three years to the day after her execution. A special elevated platform had been constructed so that as many of the crowd as possible could view the ghostly white cloth that covered the monument fall away as Queen Alexandra unveiled the monument.

Nurse Cavell's coffin arrives at Thorpe station, 15 May 1919. Her body was easily identified by the uniform she wore when it was exhumed from the firing range and returned to England to be given the honoured funeral she deserved. The Belgian Army guarded the coffin across Flanders to Ostend, where it was handed over to the Royal Navy. The destroyer *Rowena* carried it across the North Sea, and naval ratings bore it ashore at Dover. In London the coffin was drawn on a gun carriage to Westminster, and thence to Norwich, where gun carriages drew the flag-draped coffin to the cathedral.

Nurse Cavell's coffin is taken on to the shoulders of Regular Army NCOs (a number of whom she had helped escape across the frontier) to make its final journey for committal at Life's Green outside Norwich Cathedral, 15 May 1919. Prayers were read, 'Abide with me' was sung and the Bishop pronounced the blessing. The last post was then sounded and finally the *Nunc Dimittis* was sung. Her final words are recorded on a plaque by the grave: 'I have seen death so often that it is not fearful or strange to me, and this I would say, standing as I do in view of God and Eternity. I realise that patriotism is not enough. I must have no hatred or bitterness against anyone.'

Some of the girls from the fancy dress parade are joined by the servicemen representing the Army, Navy and Air Force at the Blakeney Peace Day Carnival, 19 July 1919.

A group of returned soldiers. Some of the returned servicemen of North Walsham pose in one last group photograph in Ship Yard just before their complimentary dinner in the Church Rooms, 25 July 1919. A total of 682 men went to war from North Walsham; 99 of them died in the conflict.

Between the Wars

Capt A.T.M. Berney Ficklin MC places a wreath on behalf of the British Legion at Hempnall war memorial on Remembrance Sunday, November 1926. After the 'War to end all wars' came a time to remember fallen comrades. Over 100,000 Norfolk men fought in the First World War: one in nine was killed and thousands returned handicapped in mind or body. Parades of returned servicemen in their long winter coats and variety of hats, their simple First World War medals twinkling in the winter sunshine as they marched down the street led by the village band, were familiar and poignant sights across the county. Sixty years later, even with the hindsight of the Second World War, one of them wrote: 'There can never be another war like the Great War, nor the comradeship and endurance we knew then. I think, perhaps, men are not like that now.'

Norwich street collectors for the first ever British Legion Earl Haig Fund Remembrance Day collection on 11 November 1921. It was organised by Norfolk British Legion and the Norfolk County War Pensioners Committee. The most poignant of all the flag day symbols was sold for the first time: disabled ex-servicemen had worked hard over the previous twelve months in a special factory making paper poppies. In 1921 'Poppy Day' raised £106,000 nationally for the benefit of widows, orphans and the estimated 500,000 disabled British ex-servicemen.

Staff of the Norfolk County War Pensions Committee in the Bishop's Palace grounds, Norwich, November 1921. Their workload was a heavy one as thousands of Norfolk men returned home disabled to find that there was not a 'land fit for heroes' awaiting them. Many men, because of their disabilities, could not return to their old jobs, while some could never work again, and despite the best efforts of the War Pensions Committee many disabled soldiers suffered great hardship through the 1920s and '30s.

King George V on an informal visit to the Regimental War Memorial Cottages when they were nearing completion, 2 February 1921. The cottages were paid for by donations and subscriptions as a memorial to the 6,000 officers and men who died serving in the Norfolk Regiment from 1914 to 1918. The dignitaries along the front row are, left to right, the Earl of Leicester, the Princess Royal, Lt-Col C.M. Jickling OBE, -?-, Maj Otter, HM King George V, -?-, -?-, Queen Mary and Lt-Col G.J.B. Duff MC.

Earl Haig visited the Norfolk County Mental Hospital, Thorpe, on 29 November 1921 during his two-day visit to Norwich. While at the hospital Earl Haig unveiled a plaque to commemorate the hospital's role throughout the First World War, when it treated wounded servicemen in its capacity as The Norfolk War Hospital. He is accompanied by the hospital Commandant, Lt-Col David George Thomson CBE, MD, the Lord Mayor, Mr H.N. Holmes and the Earl of Leicester.

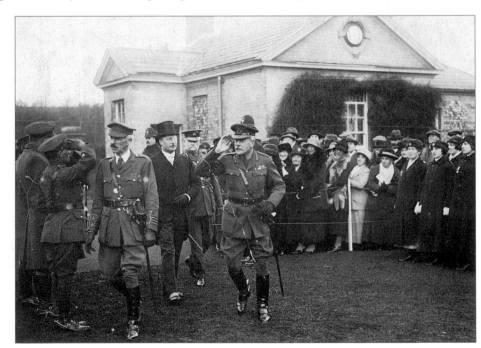

National Agricultural Labourers and Rural Workers Union meeting at Wroxham, *c.* 1920. After the First World War the returned soldiers soon found a very different life in the countryside to the one they had expected. A recession was setting in and wages were low, while increased mechanisation and technological innovation – coupled with easy importation of modern machinery from America – pushed more and more men out of work on the land. Mutual support and solidarity was the only answer to surviving the depression, so frequent public meetings, speeches and local rallies were held by agricultural labourers' unions across Norfolk.

A plough under police escort during the agricultural labourers' strike, near Castle Acre, March 1923. The recession in rural Norfolk between 1920 and 1922 saw farm labourers' wages reduced from 42s to 25s for fifty-two hours of work a week. In March 1923 over 10,000 men came out on strike. Although farmers had sympathy for the men's plight they could not afford to pay more and brought in blackleg labour. Such workmen faced the threat of their machinery being smashed, or even physical violence, so much so that police reserves were drafted in and put on escort work and patrols protecting blacklegs on farms across the county. At the end of the strike more than 200 labourers faced criminal proceedings for trespass and intimidation, but Ramsay Macdonald intervened and the men went back to work at 25s with no victimisation.

The return of the battered R33 airship to Pulham, 16 April 1925. The R33 was built by Armstrong Whitworth and first arrived at Pulham in March 1919; it was a familiar sight over the station for more than six years. During the night of 16/17 April 1925 gale force winds tore the R33 from its mooring mast. Streaming water from its ballast tanks, it drifted with a crew of one NCO, eighteen civilian airshipmen and one officer, thirty-year-old Flt-Lt R.S. Booth. The airship was blown out across the North Sea to the Dutch coast before full control could be regained. Eight hours later the vessel had limped back to England. The local and national press descended on Pulham *en masse* to greet the battered ship, its smashed nose bearing testament to the ordeal she and her crew had been through. The image hit every national newspaper. Pulham's commanding officer, Maj Scott, described the safe return flight as one of the greatest achievements of an airship. The crew were later presented with watches by King George V and the coxswain Flt Sgt 'Sky' Hunt was awarded the Air Force Medal

Herbert Duffy, the Fakenham rag and bone man, on his Fakenham Show prize-winning cart, Holt Road, 1925.

The visit of Queen Elizabeth, 1578, re-enacted by the Norwich Players: a scene from the Norwich Pageant, 21–24 July 1926. Produced by the founder of the Norwich Players and creator of the Maddermarket Theatre, W. Nugent Monck, the purpose of the pageant was to promote awareness of the historical events and characters that had shaped the city. Other scenes included Emma and the Normans (1076), Queen Philippa and the Weavers (1336), the Black Death (1349) and Charles II and Sir Thomas Browne (1671). The pageant was staged in the open air on the Newmarket Road Ground, where seating was provided for 2,000 people per performance. Tickets could be bought in advance from the Haymarket Picture Theatre, and ranged in price from 1s 3d to 10s 6d.

Widening Castle Meadow, 1927. This was once a narrow road circling Norwich's Castle Mount, but the increasing demand from all types of traffic using it prompted a widening scheme enacted between 1926 and 1927. Pedestrians were particularly happy to see this after developing a dread of being trapped between the trams and the railings as they almost scraped by on the Castle side.

Members of Tasburgh and District British Legion on Remembrance Sunday Church Parade, November 1926. The close comradeship and need for understanding and recognition of the horrors suffered by those who fought in the First World War brought about the formation of many ex-servicemen's groups. Among them were the 'Old Contemptibles' for personnel who served in 1914, the 'Better 'Ole Club' and the 'Comrades of the Great War', who not only provided a meeting point but mutual support in spirit and finance for those in need.

Bertie Withers, a private soldier from Norwich, severely wounded while serving with the 4th Battalion, the Norfolk Regiment, opens Norwich's war memorial on 8 October 1927. The fine memorial was designed by Sir Edwin Lutyens RA and was originally placed at the east end of the Guildhall.

The opening of Eaton Park by HRH Edward, Prince of Wales, 30 May 1928. Work began on the 80 acre site in 1924 to plans drawn up by Capt Sandys Winch, Superintendent of the Norwich Parks and Gardens Committee. Over the next three and a half years two thirds of Eaton Park was developed, providing labour for 103 unemployed men a week. When the park was officially opened it had six full size bowling greens, thirty-five grass tennis courts, twelve hard tennis courts, ten cricket pitches, five hockey pitches and fourteen football pitches. It was possible for as many as 600 people to take part in organised games here at any one time.

Elm Hill, Norwich, *c*. 1929. With hindsight it is inconceivable that when this photograph was taken historical Elm Hill, today's jewel in the crown of the city's street heritage, was designated a slum area. The full demolition of the area was proposed and its fate was placed on the table of the city council chamber. The vote was taken, and Elm Hill was saved by a majority of one.

Fishing trawlers, Yarmouth. The drifters are stoking up for another trip to sea and the smoke from their funnels causes a smog over Great Yarmouth, *c*. 1928. Over a thousand boats annually came to Great Yarmouth as they followed the herring shoals around the coast. It was said that when all the boats were in you could walk on their bows from Yarmouth quayside to Gorleston.

Following the boats down the coast by train came the Scots fisher girls. Nimble and hard fingered, these girls gutted fish by the thousand at incredible speed. One was timed as gutting fifty-seven fish in one minute. Even in their rest period the women kept their fingers and bodies active by walking, talking and knitting, often at the same time! After enjoying a brief revival, the industry was brought to a standstill during the Second World War. After the war indiscriminate fishing precluded any recovery, and the last of the Scottish drifters and fisher girls were seen in Yarmouth in the late 1960s.

HRH Princess Mary, Viscountess Lascelles, Commandant-in-Chief of British Red Cross Detachments, accompanied by Maj Hossack, County Officer Frank Emms and Superintendent Sidney Scott of Norwich City Lads Club Division as she inspects a guard of honour of St John Ambulance personnel from Norwich divisions. This event was part of an inspection, competitive display and prize giving for the Norfolk Red Cross detachments, which was held at Crown Point on Saturday 29 June 1929.

R101 flies over Norfolk, 1929. Leaving Cardington she flew to North Norfolk and circled the royal estate at Sandringham where King George V and Queen Mary waved to the airship as it passed overhead. The R101 then made her way along the coast to fly over Sir Samuel Hoare's house at Northrepps (Sir Samuel had earlier been Secretary of State for Air and was on board the airship that day). Moving inland she flew over Norwich in tribute to the men and women of Boulton & Paul who had carried out the detail design and made the framework for this mighty airship, which was heralded as 'A triumph of engineering'. Tragedy struck the R101 on 5 October 1930 on her maiden voyage to India, when she crashed into the north-west ridge of the Bois de Coutumes near Beauvais in northern France. Out of the fifty-four people on board only six survived.

One of Norwich's most famous landmarks is the ancient water gate known as Pull's Ferry. Taking its name from John Pull, the landlord of the adjacent inn and ferry keeper in 1796, it is seen here in 1929 during the last full year of the operational ferry's existence. Described in the 1869 history of the city as 'the roughest bit of picturesque in Norwich', this fifteenth-century watergate straddled a canal which ran up to the cathedral close until it was filled in during the late eighteenth century.

Visitors queue up to inspect the *Flying Scotsman*, centrepiece at the London & North Eastern Railway's rolling stock exhibition held at Thorpe station, 2–3 May 1931. The event, opened by Mr Russell Colman, Lord Lieutenant of Norfolk, also gave the public their first chance to see the 'hush-hush' engine, the 'largest, most up-to-date engine in all England' weighing 166 tons and measuring 76 ft long. Placed beside this great engine was one of the new smaller shunting engines, the Sentinel. They were labelled 'Dignity' and 'Impudence'.

Old Crome's Mill ablaze in the fire which destroyed it, 23 March 1933. Built in 1730 as a post mill on Mousehold Heath, Sprowston Mill was known as Old Crome's Mill after John Crome (1768–1821), artist and founder of the Norwich School of Painting, featured it in his masterpiece *A Mill on the Heath*.

HRH the Prince of Wales inspects some of the aeroplanes after he officially opened Norwich Municipal Airport near Mousehold Heath on 21 June 1933.

On the night of 13 December 1933 the 65 ton barge *Sepoy* was driven ashore 200 yards off Cromer. The motor lifeboat was attending the sailing barge *Glenway* beached at Happisburgh. It was bitterly cold and townsfolk watched with horror as *Sepoy* sank and the two-man crew climbed the rigging and lashed themselves to the mast. The call went out to raise the crew of the reserve rowing lifeboat while the rocket brigade attempted to fire a line to the barge. The wind was so strong that the lines were blown back, as was the reserve lifeboat, *Alexandra*, which was driven back by 12 ft to 20 ft high waves. The average age of her crew was sixty. By the time Cromer's lifeboat, the *H.F. Bailey*, was recalled the two men of the *Sepoy* were suffering from severe exposure. Coxswain Henry Blogg attempted to attach lines but the boats parted and the lifeboat was holed. In desperation Blogg drove the lifeboat over the sunken decks of the wreck, leaving just enough time to snatch the first crew member from the mast before the next wave carried them off. They did the whole thing again to get the skipper off. The lifeboat was damaged and short of fuel, and there was no other alternative but to make a final dangerous move – beaching at Cromer.

Norwich City FC at the Nest. A nostalgic image of Norwich City FC (left) and Grimsby Town (right) with fans crammed in stands behind. This picture was taken on Monday 7 May 1934 during the last season that 'The Canaries' played at 'The Nest'. In front of a crowd of 13,165 City beat Grimsby Town 7–2: the scorers were Jack Vinall (5) and Alf Kirchen (2). In front of the group, in the middle, is the Norfolk and Norwich Hospital Cup. To the left is City's Champion's shield for 3rd Division (South) while Grimsby display their champion's shield for Division 2. I bet they were sore at being beaten so resoundingly by City. We could certainly do with a result like that these days!

All-round favourite Tessie O'Shea (sixth from right) is welcomed along with the rest of the cast to the Theatre Royal, Norwich, ready for the opening night of their travelling entertainment show 'Radiolympia', early 1934. Beside them is the theatre's first motorised advertising van which would drive around the streets of Norwich broadcasting, over its Marconiphone speaker system, excerpts, music and details of the shows – which were performed twice nightly at 6.30 and 8.40 pm.

The Theatre Royal was well ablaze when this photograph was taken on 22 June 1934. An assistant cashier had noticed flames underneath the safety curtain and raised the alarm. Two hours later the fire, despite attempts to dowse it by Norwich City Fire Brigade and their Merryweather fire engine, had gutted the theatre in one of 'the fiercest fires ever known in the city'.

Delighted children cheer and hold up their souvenir cartons of chocolate toffees in the playground of Crooks Place School, Norwich, Friday 3 May 1935. Every schoolchild received a box of toffees and a commemorative medal from Norwich Education Authority for King George V's Silver Jubilee.

Jarrold's Corner, London Street, Norwich, was covered in bunting and decorations to celebrate the Silver Jubilee of HM King George V. Commencing on Jubilee Day, 6 May 1935, the decorations remained up for Jubilee Week and were judged by the Jubilee Committee. Three classes of prizes were offered, for best decorated business premises, private house and street. Celebrations, concerts and special events were held throughout the city: these included a grand street procession, a non-stop whist drive, a review of troops on the football field behind Britannia Barracks and a service for youth organisations at the cathedral.

The Children of Mary passing the Slipper chapel, just some of the 1,000 pilgrims who had travelled to the shrine of Our Lady of Walsingham on 14 July 1935.

The opening of Norwich City FC's new football ground on Carrow Road by Mr Russell Colman, Lord Lieutenant of Norfolk, 31 August 1935. The ceremony was watched by a crowd of 29,779 before the City went on to play West Ham United. The move to Carrow Road was brought about in 1934 when their previous ground, 'The Nest' on Rosary Road, which had served the City well since 1907, was declared unfit for second division matches by the Football Association.

It was Christmas all year round at the Caley Cracker Works on Chapel Field, Norwich, seen here *c.* 1935. It was renowned for table waters, ginger ale and beer; sales were, however, seasonal. Mr Caley did not like to 'lay off' staff during the winter so he started manufacturing cocoa in 1883, followed by chocolate in 1886. In 1897, to keep the girls who prepared frills for chocolate boxes busy in quieter times, Caley's started making crackers. By the early years of the century over 700 people were employed in chocolate and cracker manufacture and these products were exported all over the world.

A sad occasion took place in Norwich on the night of 10 December 1935, when the last ever tram service was run. It was manned by the company's most senior driver, Mr G. Hill, who was joined by their youngest employee Mr B. Fisher. The last journey was from Orford Place to the tram sheds on Silver Road: the tram was absolutely packed and those who could not find a place bought souvenir tickets. As the tram left the gathered crowd sang 'Auld Lang Syne'.

With the end of the trams came the end of the tram tracks. The small groups of workmen with their fine gravel and steaming pots of hot tar, gradually performing the laborious task of filling in the tram lines, are seen here on St Giles Street in 1936. This was to become a familiar sight on the streets of Norwich for months after the closure of the tram service.

The old rat-ridden municipal buildings have been demolished along with some of the historic buildings on St Peter's Road, *c.* 1950. In their place foundations have been dug and scaffolding and steel girders have started to rise up to become the skeleton of the new Norwich City Hall. Like the creation of the parks and council housing estates, this project was mainly devised by the Labour Norwich City Council to create work for both skilled and unskilled labourers in those depressed times.

Work continued apace on the new Norwich City Hall, and by 1938 the great bell, weighing nearly 3 tons, which had just arrived from the Croydon iron foundry where it was cast, was rolled on rods and planks into position ready to be hoisted up to the top of the 185 ft clocktower. On quiet, still nights the bell can still be heard all over the city when it chimes the hours.

The clocktower was the last feature of the new City Hall to be completed, and is seen here ready to be capped off in 1938. The last of the buildings in front of City Hall are being demolished to make way for the new site for the city's war memorial and memorial gardens which extend across the back of the Market Place.

Pictured shortly after 1,000 specially invited children had sung the National Anthem, led by the band of the 4th Battalion, Royal Norfolk Regiment, Norfolk's Chief Constable, J.H. Dain OBE, accompanies HM King George VI and HM Queen Elizabeth as they mount the steps to carry out the opening ceremony of the new Norwich City Hall on Saturday 29 October 1938. Built to the designs of architects C.H. James and S. Rowland Pierce, the whole project – including the redevelopment of the provision market and the building of the attached police and fire stations – had taken three years, and cost £222,000

A veteran of the Royal Flying Corps approaches the Norwich city war memorial to lay his fitting floral tribute on Remembrance Day 1938. He is followed by members of the Norfolk Yeomanry and representatives from a host of Norwich veterans associations and uniformed groups. This was the first service of its kind at the new war memorial and memorial gardens. The Market Place is crammed with thousands of people watching the occasion.

The Second World War

The concerned faces of the schoolmasters as they marshal the boys into the underground
shelter show that this rehearsal of air-raid drill at Norwich City School was taken very
seriously. As early as 1938 trenches were dug around the county to afford protection for the
civilian population in the event of attack from the air. More formal underground shelters were
dug in public parks in February 1939, and instructional notices from the Air Raid Precautions
(ARP) service about what to do in the event of an air raid were delivered to every household.

March past at the County Parade of St John Ambulance Brigade Divisions from across Norfolk at Eaton Park, Norwich, Sunday 11 June 1939. In the first parade of its kind in the county over 700 personnel were reviewed by Colonel J.L. Sleeman CB, Chief Commissioner of the SJAB Overseas. Among the dignitaries who accompanied him were County President Viscount Bury, County Commissioner Sir Thomas Cook and P.E. Curl Esq, Lord Mayor of Norwich.

Assembling civilian issue gas masks at Wells, 1939. Hard lessons learnt from poison gas in the First World War coupled with the anticipated air attacks like those seen during the Spanish Civil War prompted the creation of regional ARP committees across Great Britain in the mid-1930s. As war loomed the supply depots where gas masks were assembled were overloaded by sheer demand, so they concentrated their efforts on dispatching gas mask parts to be assembled in the places that requested them. All across Norfolk town and village halls were to be found filled by 'production lines' of volunteers, like these in Wells.

Evacuees from Bethnal Green and Edmonton arrive at North Walsham Market Place, 1 September 1939. War was imminent and the first evacuation of 827,000 schoolchildren, 524,000 mothers and children under school age, nearly 13,000 expectant mothers, 7,000 disabled people, and 103,000 teachers and helpers from urban areas was ordered from London and its boroughs.

Off on exercise, members of Norwich ARP service are ready to deploy their mobile decontamination carts, September 1939. Each decontamination squad consisted of six men fully suited in heavy anti-gas suits and would be needed to neutralise or remove the splashes of liquid left on walls or buildings after a gas attack, using bleaching powder.

Using a Norwich Corporation Electricity Department lorry as emergency response transport, members of Norwich ARP services in their heavy anti-gas suits move in to neutralise a gas bomb during a fire and gas demonstration at the rear of Norwich City Hall, September 1939.

The burial of Oberleutnant zur See W. Wodtke at Sheringham Cemetery, December 1939. At 3 am on Wednesday 5 December 1939 a twin-engined Heinkel III crashed on Sheringham beach. The bodies of the two crewmen were washed up shortly after on North Norfolk beaches. At this point in the conflict the horrors of war were somewhat distant. It was still a 'Gentlemen's' or 'Phoney' war, and this was typified by the treatment of the two bodies. The first to be recovered was that of the observer, Oberfeldwebel Emil Rodel, who was buried at Bircham Newton with full honours. The pilot, Oberleutnant Wodtke, was washed up later and taken to Sheringham Cemetery in a swastika-draped coffin. The Last Post was sounded, an eleven-gun salute was fired and a Flanders poppy was dropped on his coffin.

The special detachment of men from 5th Battalion, the Royal Norfolk Regiment assigned to guarding HM King George VI are photographed at Sandringham in December 1939. The winter of 1939–40 was one of the coldest on record. Inland at Sandringham the weather was very cold; for the rest of the 5th Battalion stationed at Weybourne Camp on the coast it was perishing. Weybourne was designed as a summer camp and offered very little protection from the elements. It was so cold that the sea froze and on the camp only one toilet (in close proximity to a well-fired heater) was not frozen solid.

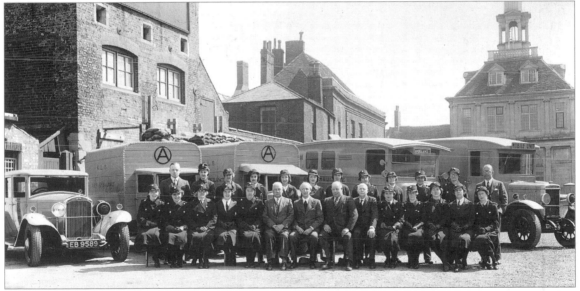

Lady ambulance drivers and senior male officials associated with local ARP services at King's Lynn, *c*. 1940. They are seated in front of the two town ambulances run under the auspices of the Joint Ambulance Committee of the British Red Cross Society and the Order of St John of Jerusalem (right) and the new ARP ambulances provided by King's Lynn Borough (left). It was estimated that the air bombing campaign over England would cause the deaths of thousands within the opening months of the war, so ambulances, mobile aid units and recovery vehicles were purchased or more likely converted to meet this terrible need. Rotas were drawn up to provide twenty-four hour cover on ambulances with women and men (who were unable to serve in the Armed Forces) trained up to drive and crew them. The blitz claimed a terrible casualty toll, but thank God the thousands of compressed cardboard coffins supplied to ambulance centres across the country were never needed

Winston Churchill, while on a visit to the east coast defences, inspects men of the 2nd Battalion, the Cambridgeshire Regiment at Holt, 7 August 1940. These men were entrusted with the task of maintaining the coastal defences in the locality and were sent out on nightly bicycle patrols to spot enemy raiders or attempted landings by parachute troops. Most of them were sent with the 18th Division to fight in the war in the Far East. Surrendered at Singapore, they were to spend the rest of the conflict in Japanese hands.

HM King George VI reviews men from the Royal Naval Patrol service and minesweepers at Gorleston as part of his review of the East Coast defences, 23 August 1940. He was received by a guard of honour from the 4th Battalion, the Royal Norfolk Regiment and WRNS, and the event was concluded with three hearty cheers for His Majesty from all on parade.

The bomb disposal officer's stethoscope is still gently held against the side of the delayed action 1,000 lb bomb as it is carefully winched from its crater on Theatre Street, Norwich, 24 September 1940. It was one of four bombs dropped during the air raid of 18–19 September 1940. One of the delayed action bombs fell on Mousehold Heath and exploded twelve hours later along with two incendiaries, causing minimal damage, while this bomb buried itself on Theatre Street, near Church Street. It damaged a gas main, thus adding to the hazards faced by the bomb disposal squad. It was defused and left for a week before it was hoisted out and taken away.

Members of 10th (City of Norwich) Battalion, having attended a cathedral service, march up Tombland past their Corps Commander, December 1940. The battalion was founded on 17 May 1940 when Lt-Col B.F. Hornor DSO was commissioned to raise a unit of Local Defence Volunteers in the city. Within three days 500 men fell in at Chapel Field Drill Hall, and twenty-four hours later nightly guards and patrols were on duty throughout the garrison area. The only problem was the acute shortage of weapons, which became so serious that old Crimean War vintage muskets were borrowed from the Castle Museum for training purposes. By July 1940 supplies were improving for the LDV and uniforms arrived just in time for their renaming as the Home Guard. At stand-down in December 1944 the battalion strength was 113 officers and 2,495 other ranks.

A YMCA van brings some comforts and certainly a hot cup of tea to the residents of bomb-damaged Walpole Street, Norwich, after the bombing raid of 18 February 1941. The damage inflicted by high explosives on this area of small houses and shops was greater than anything yet seen in Norwich. The Vauxhall Tavern was blown to pieces and the blast inflicted terrible damage on Vauxhall Street, Horace Street, Walpole Street and Coach and Horses Street, rendering 140 people homeless.

One of the wrecked houses on Cromer Road, Sheringham, after the first serious raid on the town, Sunday 22 September 1940. A total of four high explosive bombs were dropped on the Barford Road and Cromer Road area of the town. A Mrs Abbs was killed while waiting for a bus on Cromer Road and fifteen other people were injured, six of them seriously. A total of 529 properties were damaged in this one raid.

The wreckage of the Ferry Inn after a stick of bombs was dropped on Horning at 9.45 pm on Saturday 26 April 1941. It is thought a pool of light coming from the inn must have been spotted by the bomber. Fifteen bombs were dropped: the majority caused limited damage on the surrounding marshland, but four found the inn and gave it a direct hit at its busiest time. Of the twenty-four people in the bar twenty-one lost their lives, including five members of the Sutton family.

Norwich Gas Works Platoon, No. 5 Company, 10th (City of Norwich) Battalion, Norfolk Home Guard, May 1941. Their jobs at the gas works are shown in brackets. Back row, left to right: Pte E. Daynes (inspector), Pte Evans (stove repairer), Pte Vince (clerk), Pte Utting (fitter's assistant), Pte Symonds (canvasser), Pte Slipper (clerk), Pte Mount (fitter), Pte Smith (fitter's assistant), Pte Scott (inspector), Pte R. Daynes, a Lewis gunner (fitter's assistant), Pte Vincent (fitter's assistant), Pte Waller (fitter's assistant), Pte Holland (slot collector). Middle row: Pte Bealey, a Lewis gunner (retort setter), Pte Staff (coke clerk), Pte W. Wright (blacksmith), Pte R. Wright (blacksmith), Pte Goose (slot collector), Pte Mastin (clerk), Pte Williams (fitter's assistant), Pte Death (inspector), Pte Bird, a Lewis gunner (draughtsman), Pte Ward (inspector), Pte Hardy, a Lewis gunner (draughtsman), Pte Bushell (fitter), Pte Waters (fitter), Pte Horn (coal elevator), Pte Tuddenham (clerk). Front row: Pte Barker (inspector), Cpl Heugh (slot collector), Cpl Stubbs (stove shop charge hand), Cpl Bloomfield (fitter), Sgt South (syphon attendant), Sgt Dawson (service laying), Sgt Paston (slot collector), CSM Littlewood (clerk), Lt Mills (ironworker), Platoon Sgt Quantrill (showroom official), Cpl Hubbard (fitter), Cpl Clayton (fitter), Cpl King (coke ground hand), Cpl Carpenter, the Lewis Gun instructor (slot collector), L/Cpl Norton, a Lewis gunner (fitter), Pte Davison (fitter).

HM Queen Elizabeth (The Queen Mother) talks to one of the Women's Land Army girls who put on a display of tractor ploughing techniques at Sandringham, spring 1942. Begun in the autumn of 1938 after a major recruiting campaign in 1940, nationally about 85,000 ladies aged eighteen or over joined the Women's Land Army.

The scene on Rupert Street sums up the devastation suffered by the city during the 'Baedeker Blitz'. These were the worst raids on Norwich, which was targeted along with other British cities 'of significant historical interest' in an attempt to break morale on the nights of 27/28 and 29/30 April 1942. Over 297 high explosive bombs and thousands of incendiaries were dropped during those two nights of hell. A total of 231 people were killed and 689 were wounded.

HM King George VI paid a surprise visit to Norwich on Tuesday 13 October 1942 to view the damage and to meet the people affected by the blitz. During the day he toured the worst-affected areas of bombed houses and factories. His Majesty is seen here being guided around the wrecked shell of Caley's factory on Chapel Field. He also visited the cathedral, saw casualties in the Norfolk and Norwich Hospital and inspected a parade of Norwich Civil Defence workers and members of the city's emergency services.

Members of the special ARP duties section, Seventh Battalion, Norfolk Home Guard, *c.* 1943. The Seventh Battalion, covering the King's Lynn and Sandringham area, had a distinguished war record. British Empire Medals were awarded to Sgt Tipple and Cpl Smith for rescuing crews from crashed RAF planes and thirteen Certificates of Merit were issued to members of the battalion. Lt Atkins invented and produced the Atkins Mobile Mounting for the blacker bombard, and a simple but valuable anti-aircraft mounting for light machine guns was devised by Capt S. Kay and set up to great effect at key points around King's Lynn. In addition to its Home Guard duties the battalion was assigned special ARP duties and regularly fielded parties for attendance during air raids, being particularly commended for its actions when the King Edward VII School buildings were set on fire by incendiary bombs

Victory in Europe Day, Norwich, 8 May 1945. Hundreds of American servicemen, whose bases covered a great deal of Norfolk by the end of the war, march past the saluting dais on the day on which Winston Churchill said 'We may allow ourselves a brief period of rejoicing'. The parade included representatives of all the services who were present in the county during the war, including Civil Defence, emergency services and the Home Guard.

Ex-Japanese POWs, many of them from 4th, 5th and 6th Battalion, The Royal Norfolk Regiment, at Aomi Hall, Japan, August/September 1945. They had gone through hell and seen hundreds of their comrades needlessly die during the forced-labour construction of the notorious Burma–Siam railway. Most of them were just country lads, all of them Territorials, none was ever quite the same again. Colonel A.E. 'Flicker' Knights MC, MM said of them: 'In spite of all the Japanese could do, the brutality of the guards, frequent beatings, humiliation and torture suffered by the men of the 4th, 5th and 6th Battalions, The Royal Norfolk Regiment, they never forget they were soldiers. It was their steady discipline, inflexible courage through adversity and a native dignity and comradeship unique to Norfolk men that brought them through their horrific ordeal.'

The Post War Years 1945–59

Officers and men representing all battalions of the Royal Norfolk Regiment parade in front of Norwich City Hall when the Regiment was granted the Freedom of the City (the right to march through it 'with bayonets fixed, colours flying and bands playing') on 3 October 1945. The Guard of Honour was commanded by Maj David Jamieson VC, with colours carried by Lt John Lincoln MC and Capt Ernest Ridger.

Arthur H. Colman the blacksmith no doubt having a good old mardle with his waiting customers at Strumpshaw smithy in September 1945. The scene, composed in the spirit of the great rural painters like Edward Seago or Sir Alfred Munnings, is truly a timeless image of rural peace after war.

The male bus drivers and conductors at the city depot of the Eastern Counties Bus Company say farewell to the last of the wartime 'clippies' based in Norwich. At the end of the war there were about 250 of them working from the depot. The last of them, Mrs Doris Manguzi, was leaving after six years' service: she checks the waybill with her relief conductor at Castle Meadow for the last time.

First tenants of the new postwar council housing estate are presented with the keys by the Lord Mayor of Norwich, spring 1947. Identified in the 1945 City Plan as 'a completely new neighbourhood unit', the new brick houses were built on the site of the prefabricated estate put up on the old Norwich City Aerodrome. This estate became known as the 'Heartsease'.

The Wednesday auction in full swing at Norwich Corn Exchange, August 1950. The Corn Market, which was almost always held on Saturdays, was housed in St Andrew's Hall between 1796 and 1828. It became an extensive concern, and construction of the first purpose-built Corn Hall began in 1826. It was completed in 1828 for £6,000. In 1861 the old hall was demolished and a new, more commodious hall was built in its place for £17,000. Brisk trade was carried on there as were concerts and sporting events for over 100 years until it was sold for redevelopment and was demolished in 1963.

Full parade in the Grand Ring at the Royal Norfolk Agricultural Association Show on Anmer Park, 1950.

Norwich City Post Office telephone exchange, May 1951. The long line of operators at work on the switchboard dealt with an average of 22,000 telephone calls a day.

Spotlights cross on Norwich Cathedral as an encore for each day's entertainment during Norwich's Festival of Britain celebrations, 1951. National celebrations in London will be remembered for the South Bank Exhibition and the 300 ft tall pinnacle called the 'Skylon'. In Norwich the celebrations were officially opened by Princess Elizabeth on Monday 18 June. They included special cricket matches at Lakenham, Gilbert and Sullivan operettas performed at the Theatre Royal, 'Norwich through the Ages' street pageant, athletics at The Firs, special exhibitions in many public buildings and a carnival on Eaton Park.

George Humm, the Coltishall harness maker, discusses the work required to repair a leather drive belt with customer Mr C. Wells, December 1951. Mr Humm was one of a dying breed. Before the domination of motor cars almost every town and village had at least one harness maker, wheelwright and blacksmith. As the trade from horses gradually faded away these craftsmen had to turn their hands to other allied trades. Harness makers made leather goods or cobbled, while blacksmiths began to turn their hands to engineering and motors, and wheelwrights to domestic woodwork. In most cases nobody took their place when they retired and their workshops, each with its own unique character, sights and smells, are lost forever.

The line-up of motor cyclists, marshals and medical attendants from the St John Ambulance Brigade at The Firs motorcycle speedway stadium, Hellesdon, Norwich, *c*. 1952. The motorcycle stars along the front row are, left to right, Jack Freeman, Billy Bales, Wal Morton, Paddy Mills, Ted Bravery, Phil Clarke and Jeff Revett.

Alec Stark and the 15¾ lb pike he caught from the lake at Sennowe Park, 8 February 1953.

HM King George VI lying in state in the church of St Mary Magdalene, Sandringham, 7 February 1952. Keeping a silent vigil around the dead King's flag-draped coffin are his gamekeepers. On the right is head keeper Howard Dodds, to the left is keeper William Clarke, and behind them are keepers Robert Amos (left) and Stanley Hooks (right).

Described in the blazing headlines of the time the 'Greatest peacetime disaster that Britain has ever known', the east coast floods happened on the fateful night of 31 January/1 February 1953. The North Sea on storm surge smashed through defences at almost 1,500 sites between Lincolnshire and Kent. This is the sleepy village of Sea Palling wrecked by tidal surge and high winds. Seven people died here.

The devastation inflicted on the fateful night 31 January/1 February may be clearly seen here at Cley as the tidal waters subside. A 2,000 million gallon torrent had swept aside the shingle bank that protected the partially reclaimed Cley and Salthouse marshes, surging into the village like a wall of water. Incredibly only one person was killed at Salthouse. This remarkable survival rate was, however, not without the considerable and courageous actions in rescues by local people and the emergency services.

At the height of the floods in King's Lynn on Saturday 31 January 1953 willing rescuers whisk girls to dry land and safety. The sea caused the Great Ouse to flood into the town, waters rose to well over 6 ft and almost 2,000 people were evacuated. In the surrounding areas the River Nar also spilled over its banks and many people were trapped in their homes unable to escape. Fifteen people from King's Lynn drowned in that night of flood horror.

In Great Yarmouth over 1,000 homes were flooded and thousands had to be evacuated, mostly from the Southtown and Cobholm area of the town. This is the queue, so reminiscent of the one in front of St Andrew's Hall after the 1912 flood (see p. 30), at the relief centre which was set up at the Southtown Drill Hall. Over the following weeks household articles, food, blankets and warm clothes, many of them sent up under the relief scheme from London, were distributed to those who had had their homes wrecked by the flood. Along the east coast more than 32,000 people were evacuated, 307 people were drowned along with thousands of farm animals and domestic pets.

Mr W.R. Barrett of Guist holding his seven-year-old mare Beauty with her ten-day-old twin foals, March 1953. On the left is Mr J. Juby of Marsham and on the right is Mr E. Colman of Foulsham, who had bred horses for more than seventy years. He could not recall twin foals being born and living before.

Group Scoutmaster Mrs S.K. Greenwood examines a souvenir pennant along with members of Langham Troop at the Coronation Jamboree of World Friendship in the Royal Park, Sandringham, Whitsun weekend, May 1953. This historic day for scouting in Norfolk was attended by over 3,000 scouts from across East Anglia and from nineteen overseas branches.

Members of the cast of *Out of the Blue* in their final number at the opening night performance at the Summer Theatre, Cromer, Monday 29 June 1953. Starting their tenth summer season, the Out of the Blue Concert Party were not in their familiar Pavilion Theatre at the end of the pier because the pier was undergoing maintenance following storm damage. As a result the Parish Hall was converted at lightning speed by Cromer Urban District Council into the Summer Theatre so the show could go on.

Miss Hazel Cook of Sennowe Park dressed as page to King Charles I at the North Elmham Pageant, 18 July 1953. Organised by the vicar, the Revd E.J.G. Ward and staged on the manor house lawn, the pageant depicted historical events and characters connected with the village over the years – from Roman times in AD 411 through the Danes, Bishop Despenser, Henry VIII and Charles I (who stayed at the village in 1621). The last scene was the news of victory at Waterloo where Lord Sondes (played by Mr F. Stebbings) ordered a celebration in the village. This announcement was met by torrents of rain, and the ensuing thunder and lightning put paid to the final grand parade and swept the kings, queens and spectators under cover. The event raised about £135 for the church repair fund.

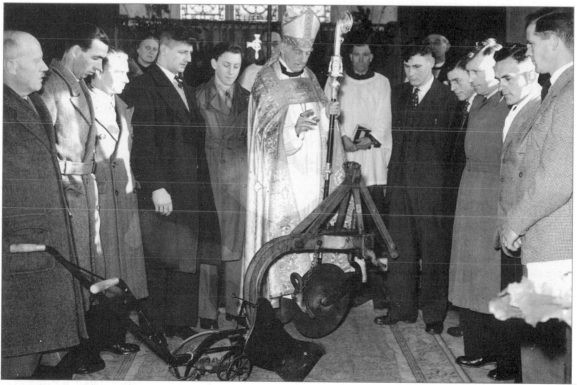

Percy Mark Herbert, Bishop of Norwich (1942–59), blessing the plough at the Plough Sunday service, St Mary the Virgin Church, Itteringham, 24 January 1954. Plough Sunday and Monday (the first Monday after Twelfth Day) commemorate the putting of plough to soil and cutting the first furrow of the year; they are steeped in emblematical folklore and country tradition. At the turn of the century Plough Mondays were marked annually with a village celebration, when newly 'initiated' plough boys dressed as scarecrows or 'mawkins' with blackened faces would take a 'fool plough' round the village and threaten to plough up the doorstep or garden path of anyone so ungenerous as to refuse them money.

Here's an unusual helper for Great Yarmouth-based reed thatcher John Jefford in July 1954. Mr Jefford's terrier, Karah, happily climbed up and down steep angled ladders with ease and patiently sat on the roof ridges to 'hand' materials to her master. I wonder if she could manage to bring up a cup of tea.

The 3rd Battalion Coldstream Guards Corps of Drums marches down Guildhall Hill heading a parade of members of Norfolk and Suffolk Branches of the Coldstreamers Association on their way to Norwich Cathedral on Sunday 26 June 1955. The Coldstreamers were led by Gen Sir Charles Loyd, Lieut-Col J.M. Langley from Ipswich and CSM Peter Wright of Blythburgh who won the VC with the Coldstream Guards during the Second World War. After the service there was a march past on Tombland where the Lord Mayor took the salute.

Country shows have always been popular showcases for rural crafts and traditional skills since the days of the Holkham Sheep Shearing Festivals at the beginning of the nineteenth century. Here we see Mr G. Roberts of Costessey Lodge and Mr W. Hobbs (Royal Army Veterinary Corps) from Melton Mowbray competing in Class 1 Shoeing Agricultural Heavy Horse at the most prestigious of all our county's shows, The Royal Norfolk Agricultural Association Show, on 27 June 1955.

The aftermath of the Cromer election, 27 May 1955. The votes are packed into mailbags before being sent for storage in the Tower of London for a year and a day.

The final phase of redevelopment for Thorpe station forecourt, *c.* 1956. Shortly after the nationalisation of the railways a general improvement scheme was begun at Thorpe station. In 1955 the remnants of the old tram lines which once served the station were taken up along with the old stone setts. The area was developed to accommodate the growing number of cars parking there, and to allow the flow of buses through the forecourt.

A scene from *Richard II* was performed at the Maddermarket Theatre, 16–24 March 1956.

It's all go at the new BBC Broadcasting House on All Saints' Green, Norwich, 4 October 1956. Here the sound engineer Mr M. Corry watches from the control desk as a broadcast is made from the studio (seen through the glass panel). All programmes went through control bays, were amplified and then sent over GPO lines to transmitters.

Station Officer R.S. Mitchell (centre) and the collectors at Fakenham Fire Brigade flag day in aid of the National Fire Services Benevolent Fund Orphans Appeal, 20 July 1957.

Caister lifeboat on the beach, with its crew led by Coxswain J.R. Plummer on board for the service to mark the centenary of the lifeboat in Caister, 27 July 1957. Capt the Hon. W.M. Wyndham-Quin, Chairman of the RNLI's Management Committee, paid tribute to the Caister boats which had saved 1,765 lives over the previous 100 years, and the twelve crew members who had received RNLI medals (one gold, the rest silver). Sir Edmund Bacon, Lord Lieutenant of Norfolk, presented the Centenary Vellum Certificate to Mr M.C. McAvoy, Secretary of the Caister branch, and a certificate of service was presented to former coxswain Joseph Woodhouse, whose family had been involved with the boat throughout its 100 years. He joined the lifeboat in 1910 and was coxswain between 1935 and 1950.

Girls lifting carrots on a field by the side of the Gayton–Litcham road, Massingham, 22 October 1957.

Sir Barry Jackson gives an address after unveiling the plaque to Nugent Monck, 11 September 1954. Nugent Monck (1878–1958) was the founder of probably the most famous repertory theatre in all England – The Maddermarket, home of The Norwich Players. He was frequently asked to take shows on tour to which he emphatically replied: 'We stay here in our own theatre and if people want to see us they will make the pilgrimage.' The theatre is still going strong today with many performances which maintain the best Monck's noble traditions.

The members of the 1958/9 Norwich City FC FA run 'dream team' in front of the old wooden main stand. Right to left: Ron Ashman (captain), Roy McCrohan, Terry Allcock, Sandy Kennon, Terry Bly, Jimmy Hill, Bobby Brennan, Matt Crowe, Errol Crossan and Barry Butler. Absent is Bryan Thurlow who was away doing his National Service. After a series of classic matches they had earned the Canaries a place in the semi-final of the FA cup, only the third 3rd Division club to achieve that. The match was against Luton at White Hart Lane on 14 March 1959. It ended 1–1, and in the replay on 18 March at St Andrew's, Birmingham, the Canaries sadly lost 1–0.

The foundations are laid for St Augustine's Swimming Pool, Norwich, September 1959. Built on the site of the bombed-out St Augustine's School, the indoor pool was designed by City Architect David Percival and built to the popular contemporary principle of enclosing the maximum amount of space with the minimum amount of material: 120 cubic yards of concrete formed the bottom of the 110 ft by 42 ft pool. Costing £161,268, it opened in March 1961 as the third largest pool in the country.

An emotional day in Norfolk's military history as the Britannia flag was lowered for the last time at Britannia Barracks, Norwich, 29 August 1959. The grand old cap badge had been worn by men of the 9th Foot, the Norfolk Regiment and the Royal Norfolk Regiment since it was granted to the regiment by Queen Anne after its outstanding bravery at the Battle of Almanza in 1707. A government white paper had suggested the restructuring and amalgamation of many of the grand old county regiments. The Royal Norfolk Regiment was amalgamated with the Suffolk Regiment to become the 1st East Anglian Regiment; today it has been embodied with other East Anglian regiments to become the Royal Anglian Regiment, and is changing yet again to become the East of England Regiment.

The Swinging '60s & '70s

The barrelling department of Bullard's Anchor Brewery, St Miles Bridge, Norwich, 1960. This brewery was founded by Richard Bullard and Richard Watts in 1837. Richard Watts dissolved the partnership in 1847 and from that time Bullard's was truly a family run business. Selling popular beer all over the county, the brewery soon acquired further adjacent properties and expanded. By 1937 Mr Gerald Bullard, a fourth-generation descendant of the founder, had joined the board after a stint in the Royal Navy: he returned just after the Second World War and took over as Chairman. He saw Bullard buy out Youngs Crawshay and Young's brewery on King Street in 1958; joining resources with S&P they bought out Morgan's in 1961. Despite these acquisitions, Bullard's still could not compete with the big national breweries and both Bullard's and S&P were bought by Watney's. In 1966 the Anchor Brewery was closed. Today it is a trendy complex of apartments and houses.

Staff of the corner shop, West End Street, Norwich, March 1961. The combined service to Bassingthwaite's Stores Ltd, grocers and wine merchants, shared by the gentlemen on this photograph was almost 200 years. Bassingthwaite's could trace its history back to the late 1880s when Frederick Henry Bassingthwaite was a grocer and sub-postmaster at 39 West End Street. The business grew and grew to occupy not only 39 but 41, 43 and 45 West End Street. Left to right: Mr W.T. Chadwick, who retired in 1940 after being manager for nearly fifty years; Mr Cyril Percy Bassingthwaite, son of the founder, who was born on the premises in 1890; Mr J.E. Bassingthwaite, grandson of the founder; and Mr E. Wright, the manager.

Civil Defence Rescue team, helped by members of the Auxiliary Fire Service, lower a 'casualty' to safety in Exercise 'Return Match' in March 1961. CD volunteers from all over Norfolk and Oxfordshire joined forces for a full-scale weekend exercise in post-atomic rescue operations. The 220 men and women who took part had to imagine that a one megaton nuclear weapon had exploded over Horsham St Faith and that the blast had destroyed most of Norwich north of the river. To bring realism over 100 casualties were made up to simulate people suffering from the after effects of nuclear blast. Oxfordshire members acted as reinforcements to the Norwich area, for the exercise postulated that the city's division was at low strength and nearing exhaustion because of the effects of radiation.

Mrs Mervyn Pike, the Assistant Postmaster General, visited Norwich to inaugurate the Norwich Postal Fortnight on 17 July 1961. She inspected Norwich's postal operations, and is seen here discussing the proposed sorting office of the future with Mr J.L. Fryer, Norwich's Head Postmaster.

The Everard tug *Stalker* carefully manoeuvres the motor vessel *Sultan* through Carrow Bridge, Norwich, 28 February 1962. The 170 ft coaster had discharged a cargo of coal and was too big to swing round in the turning basin. She was towed stern first down Carrow Reach, and there was a brief hold up at the rail swing-bridge for trains entering and leaving Thorpe station. At Trowse Eye, with the help of a stern spring and a few gentle nudges from *Stalker*, the ship was turned and set off down the Yare.

Mr H. Dibble working on the bronze bust of Henry Blogg GC at the Morris Singer Foundry in Kennington, London, April 1962. The bust was sculpted by James Woodford RA, and crafted as a monument to the greatest hero in the history of the Royal National Lifeboat Institution. Henry Blogg was Coxswain of Cromer lifeboat for thirty-eight years, with fifty-eight years' service in all (see also p. 71). In his time he went out with the boat 387 times and, with his crew, saved 873 lives. No other lifeboatman has won as many medals as Henry Blogg. He won the RNLI gold medal three times and the silver four times; he was also awarded the George Cross and the British Empire Medal. A modest man who disliked any fuss over his gallant deeds, he would rarely wear his medals or talk of his rescues. His sculpted bust faced the sea on top of the Cromer cliffs by the Coastguard House for many years after it was unveiled until the last few years when, because of vandalism, Henry's bust has been taken into the lifeboat house at the end of the pier for safe keeping.

The unmistakable presence of presenter, the late, great Dick Joice is in the foreground as the studio prepares to go on air with the 500th edition of *About Anglia* on 14 December 1962. This award-winning news magazine programme, which at its height attracted more than a million viewers, began in May 1960. Many household names worked on the programme, including Sir David Frost, who began his career with the show, David Dimbleby, antiques expert John Bly and sports presenter Steve Rider.

Norwich City firemen tackle a 'blaze' at their own headquarters, 26 March 1963. It was a well-enacted exercise for HM Inspector of Fire Brigades, Mr S.H. Carters. With him was Andrew Ryrie, the Lord Mayor of Norwich: together they inspected about fifty full-time firemen and twenty-five AFS members before the Lord Mayor pressed the alarm and smoke flares were lit in the upstairs room and on the roof of the station. Observed by members of the City Watch Committee and the Town Clerk, Mr Gordon Tilsley, four engines raced round via Bethel Street and St Giles to the station where the flares were well alight. One man was rescued from the roof and other firemen put on breathing apparatus to enter the upper rooms of the building.

German aircrew of No. 72 (Intercepter Day Fighter) Wing flying F-86 Sabre fighters were photographed on landing from Germany at RAF Coltishall, as part of a NATO exchange visit, 23 July 1963.

Have you ever seen a bull in a china shop? Shoppers on Magdalen Street in Norwich certainly did when Colin Newlove took his bull shopping on 1 July 1964. Not just any bull, William was a well-trained entertainer who had been appearing at the Royal Norfolk Show doing, among other tricks, a jump through a blazing hoop.

Wednesday 15 July 1964, and the barley harvest is away to a record early start with John Carter of Ridlands Farm, Briston, who is seen harvesting an 18-acre field of Union winter barley. In previous years it hadn't been possible to get this harvest in before mid-September. Mr Carter put the early crop down to his drilling and seeding during the first week in October, and the hardy nature of Union. The yield was 30 cwt an acre; most of the crop was sold for malting. Other farmers enjoying an early harvest were C.A.P. Hardy of Banham and Oliver Anderson of Shipdam. One Norfolk farmer, whose records went back thirty years, had noted 27 July as the earliest previous date for barley harvest, way back in 1939.

Norwich City College – East Anglia's only catering school, November 1964. This is the main kitchen where Mr D. Greenwood, Chief Cookery Instructor, and Mr R.M.C. Stewart, responsible for administration and organisation, are training students to serve lunch. One of 120 catering training centres, Norwich City College taught 'professional cooking', as well as restaurant control, hygiene, book keeping, food costing, bar and cellar work. This type of training was new to educational establishments. In pre-war Britain the restaurant business was a dependable music hall joke, but after the war customers demanded better treatment and were willing to pay. This need could only be met by more formal training. Within a few years the restaurant and hotel business had grown to become the fourth largest industry in the country.

All classes of farm animals gather in the grand ring for their final parade at the Wayland Show, 1965. A number of well-established weekend agriculture-based shows, some of which have evolved from earlier farming festivals, are held across Norfolk. They are always worth a visit as many show locally based crafts and trades not seen at larger events. Some of the most popular include the Aylsham Show, the Holkham Show, Worstead Festival and the Tunstead Trosh.

The first honorary degrees were awarded by the University of East Anglia on 23 April 1966. Here Norwich's literary doyen Ralph Mottram is presented with the honorary degree of Doctor of Letters from the Chancellor of the UEA, Lord Franks. Ralph Mottram was author of over ten history books, many reflecting aspects of Victorian Norfolk life. My favourite of his books are *If Stones Could Speak*, his authoritative, yet affectionate look at the historical remnants around us in the city of Norwich, and of course his classic *The Spanish Farm*, recalling his time at war in France 1914–19. Ralph Mottram died in 1971, and a fine tribute was paid in an obituary by his friend Eric Fowler (the *EDP*'s Jonathan Mardle). Part of it reads: 'It feels as if a whole chapter of the history of Norwich and indeed England has gone with him. Nobody else in this city will ever know or express quite so much as he did about the spirit of the place.'

Flood waters at Denver, September 1968. Heralded on Saturday 14 September with a terrible thunder and lightning storm, the heavens opened and one of the worst rain storms ever to hit the county ensued. It seemed to rain all Sunday, and by Monday Norfolk was almost at a standstill as vast areas of low-lying land were under water: rivers burst their banks and landslides blocked roads, while livestock and cars were swept away. Many areas saw the most rainfall in one day since the great downpour of 1912.

The life-line, a vital part of a frogman's equipment, is clearly shown by PC Olly Mantle, a member of the Norfolk Police underwater search and recovery unit. With him, fully 'suited up' for action, is PC James Fulton.

November 1969, and the new post office uniforms are introduced to Norfolk. On the left, Geoffrey Bowman is seen in the new postman's uniform; on the right, Mr Rodney Buckenham is wearing the old uniform, which was to be phased out over the ensuing twelve months. The new uniforms differed in being single breasted rather than double, grey instead of dark blue, and they were made of Terylene and worsted instead of wool serge.

A fire at Garlands Department Store, London Street, Norwich, 1 August 1970. The blaze began with a chip pan fire at 5 pm. The alarm was raised and three fire engines were sent out on a routine call from Bethel Street fire station. The area in which Garlands stood has always been regarded as a high fire risk, and before the first engine arrived the order was flashed to the station 'make pumps four': this was no routine call; the whole shop was burning down. Before long over seventy firemen from all over Norfolk were battling to stop the blaze spreading through the whole of historic London Street. Quite a crowd was drawn on to the Castle Mound to observe the blaze. It took over three hours to bring the fire under control. Garlands Store, which could trace its history back to 1862 in Norwich, was closed for three years of reconstruction and refurbishment. It rose like a phoenix from the embers after the fire, but sadly in 1984 it closed for good.

Norman Peak, geologist and city chalk mines expert, examines Sprowston lime kiln in January 1971. During the fifteenth and sixteenth centuries extensive mining activity occurred around and under the city of Norwich. Chalk was extracted and taken to these and other kilns to be burned to create lime for the building and tanning trades. As the city grew the maze of mines was widely forgotten, until 1824 when they were rediscovered by a group of workmen sinking a well near St Giles Gates. Their potential was realised, and the 'Underground Streets of Norwich' (radiating from the Earlham Road area) were in part lit by gas lamps, and lantern tours were available as a popular Sunday afternoon entertainment until the tunnels were judged too dangerous. Many were blocked and closed off, but children who lived in houses with cellars near the tunnels could often find an entrance, and could play in the street under the street.

A grand display for the opening night of Billy Russell's Circus Spectacular at Great Yarmouth Hippodrome, 29 May 1971. This is Josephine, the first Rumanian artiste to appear at the Hippodrome; she is suspended by her hair while juggling with flaming torches. Also featuring on the bill under the direction of Ringmaster Roberto Germains were Alan Alan the escapologist, Mary Chipperfield's African elephants, the Trio Cotez acrobats and the Doors sisters, who performed balancing acts while propelling themselves along on huge white balls.

Norwich's new Odeon cinema, opened on 8 July 1971. A preview tour was given a few days before, so that dignitaries could inspect 'the most modern and best cinema in Britain' with 'psychedelic lights' on the main staircase and 'invisible flushing arrangements' in the toilets. It was opened by 'Miss Odeon', nineteen-year-old Miss Mary Flegg of Norwich, who was chosen after a competition in the *Eastern Evening News*. The films showing on the opening night were *The Art of Self Defence* and *Symphony Hour*, Disney films which had been shown on the opening night of the old Odeon in 1938 when the cheapest seats were 6d. The main feature on this new opening night was *Valdez is Coming* starring Burt Lancaster: seats were priced at 40p stalls, 50p centre stadium and 60p rear stadium.

Norwich City Greyhound Stadium, Boundary Park, Hellesdon, just after its final closure was announced on Saturday 7 August 1971, after almost forty years of dog racing on the site. It was opened in October 1932 by William Hurrell, at a cost of £28,000. The last race was run at 9.21 pm, and was won by Madam's Daughter at 7–2. The announcement was made by Denis Pine, Managing Director of Norwich City Stadium Ltd. The last bets had been won or lost, and the traps closed for the last time.

On the steps of City Hall, Princess Anne leaves after luncheon with the mayor during her visit on Friday 14 January 1972. She apologised, with her distinctive good humour, on her arrival for being six months late. She had originally agreed to visit earlier but had been taken into hospital for a minor operation. Wearing the uniform of St John Ambulance Brigade Commandant-in-Chief for the first time, her first duty was to open the new Norfolk St John Ambulance headquarters on King Street. Her Royal Highness then went on to inspect the St John guard of honour at the Lads Club. After luncheon she attended a service in the cathedral where she enrolled 100 cadets.

The scene at Thorpe station as British Rail workers are on a work-to-rule go-slow, 17 April 1972. Local rail services were under threat to cease after 2 pm on 18 April as adequate manning of signals would become impossible. All main line services were cancelled and passengers were stranded all over the country. Emergency government and TUC action to suspend industrial action and have a 'cooling off' period were needed before some semblance of rail services could be restored over the following weeks.

Flooded shops on Bunnett Square, Colman Road, Norwich, 1 August 1972. With cool northerly winds and cold air over eastern England, conditions were ripe for severe storms. 5.51 inches of rain fell on Old Costessey, most of it in just two hours. Mr Donald Allen, manager of Baker's, the butchers, had about 6 inches of water in his shop; although minor flooding had occurred before, this was 'the worst yet' in his thirty-five years of experience.

The victorious dwile-flonking team of the Stracey Arms, Tunstall, pictured in action at the Ferry Inn, Horning, during the final of the Broadland dwile flonking championship, September 1972. This is a traditional rural sport which involves twisting a wet piece of material around a pole – but that description does not do it justice! Eight teams from Watney's Anglia Taverns throughout Broadland took part in this particular competition over a month. The Stracey Arms beat King's Head Wroxham 'A' team in the final. In the winning team was the only girl in the competition, eighteen-year-old barmaid Julie Burgess of Cantley. The winners received seven pint cans of beer each, pint tankards from Player's No. 10 and the grand trophy presented by Mr Sydney Hornigold, General Manager of Anglia Taverns – an inscribed chamber pot from which each contestant had to drink.

Mrs Shirley Jean Adye cuts the ribbon and sends the champagne bottle crashing on the bows of Caister's new volunteer lifeboat, which carried her name, Sunday 5 August 1973. Just four years after the RNLI closed the station in Caister the village had a full-size lifeboat again. The lifeboatmen and their supporters led by 'Skipper Jack' Woodhouse, had formed the Caister Volunteer Rescue Service to keep the flag flying with smaller boats until they managed to raise enough money to have a proper boat again. The boat was dedicated in a service on the beach by the Revd J.R. Lusty, Minister of Caister Beach Road Methodist church, assisted by the Rector of Caister, the Revd R.R. Dommett, with the Great Yarmouth Salvation Army Citadel Band providing music for the hymns. After the dedication Caister Coxswain Alfred 'Mobby' Brown and his crew, with rescue service officials, took the *Shirley Jean Adye* to sea and put on a fine display with an Air Sea Rescue helicopter.

Norwich traffic wardens go mobile on lightweight motor cycles, 19 September 1973. Wardens Victor Cooper, Leslie Tylee and Anthony Howard prepare to leave Bethel Street police station, but not before sharing a few words with Senior Traffic Warden Ronald Breddy. The idea behind the bikes was to allow regular patrols to outlying areas of the city, such as the no-waiting areas on Bluebell Road and Plumstead Road East.

'Heya got a loight boy?' It's Alan Smethurst, 'The Singing Postman', at the Top Rank Bingo Club in Norwich, September 1973. His broad Norfolk ditties and songs shot him to fame in 1965, when he released two EPs about his childhood near Sheringham.

The demolition of the old cooper's shop at the rear of the old Steward & Patteson Pockthorpe Brewery on Barrack Street, Norwich, 28 November 1974. Section by section the building was reduced to rubble by a 28 cwt solid steel weight suspended from a crane and wielded with deadly accuracy. The cooper's shop was one of the last buildings to be demolished on the 4½ acre site by the contractors F.W. Shepherd & Sons. The site, purchased by Norwich City Council, took about six months to be fully cleared. It was then used for the council housing and flat developments we see today.

An unusual sight was to be found among the reed beds of Hickling in February 1976. These had been harvested for centuries by scythe and hand, but in 1976 a giant Scandinavian-built reed harvester was employed to cut, bundle and cart the reeds. With its four great wheels with 3 ft wide tyres it was able to cross the boggy marshes with ease, even when carrying 2 or 3 tons of weight. In under an hour this harvester could cut 340 bundles of reed: I wonder what the marshmen of old would have made of that!

South Quay flooded at Great Yarmouth, 2 January 1976. A horrific storm blew across the county, with winds as high as 104 mph recorded. Trees and chimneys were brought down, with flying debris everywhere, while Norwich and King's Lynn were partially cut off and local emergency services were stretched to the limit. In Great Yarmouth South Quay flooded, a woman was taken to hospital after being blown across Hall Quay and at least five plate-glass windows in large department stores were blown in around the town centre.

Norwich Spring Bank Holiday fête on Ealham Park, Monday 31 May 1976. Noel Edmonds fronts the Radio One Roadshow in front of a crowd of almost 22,000. Other events on the park, all part of the action-packed 'Snap '76' programme, including an inflatable giants wrestling match between Mighty Mick and Terrible Ted, a trapeze act by Leone and Tarniya on top of an 80 ft pole, and a medieval joust and fayre, complemented by a horrifically realistic witch burning carried out by the Norfolk Royalist Society.

Here's a young John Wilson, now a familiar television fishing programme presenter, in front of his new shop on Bridewell Alley, Norfolk, June 1974. A Londoner by birth, John had been fishing in Norfolk for over twenty years and bought his first fishing tackle shop in Norwich at 18 Bridewell Alley in 1969 from Bill Cooper. Five years on he moved to larger premises – next door! John is examining a magnificent stuffed pike; another pike hung over the shop along with the brass dolphin Bill Cooper had bought when he started business forty years previously. The ironwork for the sign was by Ted Curl of Elm Hill and the woodwork by Joe Royale – two of the real old craftsmen of Norwich. Sadly the brass dolphin was stolen a few years ago and the wooden pike was taken away for 'restoration', never to be seen again.

Over 200 workers from K Group shoe factories on the march to Stuart Hall, Norwich, Tuesday 5 October 1976. They organised a 'sit in' at the firm's two factories on Northumberland Street and Sussex Street in protest at the proposed closure of one of the factories and the suggested 350 redundancies.

Preparing for just one of thousands of parties to mark Queen Elizabeth II's Silver Jubilee: over 300 jubilee mugs arrived at one of the organiser's homes before the Tuckwood Estate festivities in Norwich, May 1977.

Visit of HM Queen Elizabeth II to Norwich, 11 July 1977. On her Jubilee tour of Great Britain Her Majesty landed in a red, white and blue plane at Norwich Airport. After a drive around the street of Norwich, which were lined with flag-waving crowds, she visited the Hewett School where she was entertained by 2,500 school children from all over Norfolk with an exuberant display of dancing. After lunch at County Hall she left to carry on her tour with a visit to Ipswich.

Stubble burning at West Bilney, September 1977. Once a common sight across the county, this farming process of disposing of stubble after the harvest is now confined to our recent past. The image was almost sinister; Norfolk's recently golden, swaying fields, their yields gathered in, were ritually put to the torch and great palls of grey-black smoke would then billow up out of the blazing fields across clear blue skies.

Someone's lost their 'Chopper', the undoubted classic bicycle for children growing up in the 1970s. Seen leaning against the rack, it was just one of many bicycles awaiting recovery by its rightful owner from Norwich's Bethel Street police station store in December 1977. With the bicycles is Detective Constable Barry Leggett, who was heading the initiative to stamp out bicycle theft in the city at the time.

'Oh no it's Selwyn Froggitt', alias Bill Maynard (now known to a new generation as Claude Greengrass, the likeable yokel rogue from ITV's *Heartbeat* series), who was playing Simple Simon along with George Lacy as Dame Durden, the Patton Brothers as the giant's henchmen and Melanie Peck as Jack in the 1977 hit pantomime *Jack and the Magic Beanstalk* at the Theatre Royal, Norwich. In one classic part of the show Bill had supposedly been shopping, and wheeled a supermarket trolley of groceries on to the stage, proceeding to throw, tip and present these contents to members of the audience, much to everybody's amusement.

High winds ferociously lashed the East Anglian coast on 11 January 1976. A rapidly deepening weather depression had moved across England to the Netherlands, developing northerly gales behind it. Combined with low pressure, it also caused a tidal surge which was greater than that of 1953, but this time the coast defences held. Some of the great waves crashed over the first wave of sea defences, smashing moored boats and yachts: this one was thrown on to the quayside in front of the Pop Inn at Wells. There was widespread flooding in Norfolk coastal areas. Families at King's Lynn, Hunstanton, Burnham Overy Staithe and Blakeney were forced to evacuate their homes.

Her Majesty Queen Elizabeth, the Queen Mother is accompanied by the Revd D. Lang of St Margaret's Church, King's Lynn, on her visit to the town to view the damage caused by the floods, January 1978. In King's Lynn the flood levels in some areas were the highest ever recorded. Luckily nobody was killed, but the tidal surge up the River Ouse poured over the defences into the town. Flooding was extensive as far as Wisbech, and the cost of repairing damage in King's Lynn alone was conservatively estimated at £5.5 million.

In go the hops at the Norwich Brewery brewing hall, March 1979. We had seen all the great names in Norfolk brewing, such as Steward & Patteson, Lacon's, Young's, Crawshay & Young's, Morgan's and Bullard and Morgan's come and go. At the time the photograph was taken this was the county's only remaining operative brewery. It was founded on a worthy site, as beer had been brewed here on King Street for over 700 years. The Norwich Brewery, employing a workforce of 600, used the same traditional brewing ingredients as those who had brewed on the site all those years before: malt from East Anglian maltings, yeast, East Anglian-grown and -produced sugar and pure water from the brewery's own well 250 ft below King Street.

The Broadland Singers performing at Norwich Union's Marble Hall on Surrey Street, part of the triennial Norwich and Norfolk Music Festival, October 1979. At this sell-out performance the Broadland Singers, conducted by Angela Dugdale, delighted the audience with a recital that included Britten's Choral Dances from 'Gloriana' and part songs by Delius. Sustained applause was received for 'The Lover's Ghost' by Vaughan Williams. The performance was completed by two encores of West Country Folk Songs.

Modern Times
1980–99

In 1990 we saw the introduction of the 'Poll Tax', one of the most unpopular taxes in post-war years. It was understandably met with stiff opposition across the country. In North Walsham, the town where the 1381 Peasants' Revolt against the poll tax was crushed by soldiers under the command of Bishop Henry de Spencer, the standard was raised by the common man again, and a march in protest at this tax progressed, peaceably, through the town on Sunday 13 May 1990.

Five of Anglia Television's well-known personalities celebrate twenty-one years of Anglia Television at Anglia House, 24 October 1980. Left to right: Helen McDermott, Patrick Anthony, Christine Webber, Graham Bell and Pam Rhodes. Anglia Television went on air at 4.15 pm on 27 October 1959, the first independent television service for the people of eastern England. The original board, under its Chairman Lord Townshend of Raynham, included a wide variety of local business and media interests, among them Sir Robert Bignold, the Chairman of Norwich Union, Aubrey Buxton, the well-known traveller and conservationist, and William Copeman, head of the *Eastern Daily Press*. The first programme was called *Introducing Anglia* where Drew Russel, Newman Sanders and Colin Bower took viewers on a tour of the region with views of the countryside shot from a helicopter. Many of us have grown up with Anglia TV; I wonder how many of you remember some of the local programmes and personalities like Michael Hunt the weatherman, newscasters Caroline Raison and John Bacon, *Romper Room*, *Chatterbox*, *Bygones*, *Farming Diary* and of course *Tales of the Unexpected*.

The opening night of the Norwich Puppet Theatre, 1 December 1980. After a number of years of hope and fund-raising the project, led by distinguished puppeteers Ray and Joan Da Silva, became a reality. The little theatre was based in the redundant St James's Church on Barrack Street. Pictured shortly before curtain up, Norwich's Lord Mayor, Eric Hartley, tries his skill as a puppeteer; he is flanked by Ray and Joan Da Silva. The first production was *Humbug, Humbug*, an interpretation of Dickens's *A Christmas Carol*. It ran until 21 December, to be followed by *Pinocchio*. There have been continuous productions enjoyed by thousands of children at the theatre ever since.

During the evening of Saturday 25 April 1981 freak storms with torrential rain and 90 mph winds hit Norfolk, causing extensive flooding in the Waveney Valley and along the Bure between Buxton and Aylsham. The ten residents of Mash Row in Aylsham were evacuated by local police when water surged to their homes across Millgate as the River Bure burst its banks. Water here was 2 ft deep and possessions could only be rescued by boat. The photograph shows Mrs Clough of 3 Mash Row in front of her house in the rescue boat.

On yer bike! Community policing brought about the reinstatement of the bobby on the bike in Norwich on Monday 4 May 1981. Here we see PC Peter Robinson (left) and PC John Nobbs going out on their first patrol from Bethel Street police station on the new bikes.

The end of an era. On 10 September 1982 one of the familiar sights of Norwich was taken from his post after what must be one of the longest sentry duties in history – 162 years. He was of course the magnificent figure of an officer from the 42nd Regiment – 'The Black Watch' – who was placed in front of Miller's tobacconist at 37 London Street, Norwich in 1820; Mr Miller had founded the business in 1812. The purpose of the figure was to denote the shop as a high-quality tobacconist who sold snuff. He only left his post twice – once to be repainted and once when London Street was paved. Our Highlander is seen here with Mrs Elsie King, shop manageress (right) and Mrs Edna Rouse. Since the closure of the shop the next day the whereabouts of the snuff-taking officer have not been known, despite lively correspondence in local newspapers and a lot of amateur detective work.

One of the ruined cliff edge buildings at Hemsby following the washing this coastal area received on 1 February 1983. High seas topped the sea walls and flooded the coast road at Walcott, and an old people's home had to be evacuated. Some residents along the coast road were also evacuated to the holiday village at Ostend where they were given tea by the ladies' section of the Walcott Flood Emergency Committee. Offers of help came from the WRVS and members of Stalham WI turned up at the centre. Other residents decided to stay put, their houses and bungalows surrounded by sandbags and up to 2 ft of water.

Although the floods of 1 February were bad they would have been far more disastrous if the multi-million pound flood defences had not been in place. There was still a great deal of clearing up to do. Here are some of the sixteen WRVS members from Stalham, Sutton and Smallburgh manning an emergency refreshment centre in Walcott village hall for workers who were clearing away storm debris. Left to right: Mrs Dorothy Fawcett, Mrs Jean Burton, Mrs Valerie Moore, North Norfolk District Emergency Services Officer for the WRVS, and Mrs Nell Cripps.

A colourful pageant graced Norwich's historic Elm Hill on Saturday 7 July 1984. This was the Norwich Dragon Parade. About thirty dragons made by schools from across Norfolk mustered at The Garth behind St Andrew's Hall and processed around Princes Street and Elm Hill. The dragons ranged from one occupant to eighteen children, who each made up a segment of the beast's body. The parade was part of the 'Second City' celebrations, which aimed to recapture some of the atmosphere of the medieval processions. It was organised by Mrs Enid Stephenson of the Hungate Bookshop and was well attended by civic dignitaries, including the Lord Mayor, Stan Peterson, accompanied by his two ceremonially costumed 'Whifflers', played by local naturalist Ted Ellis and David Cuffley, the *Eastern Evening News* 'Whiffler' writer.

A dramatic 'rescue' is staged between Cromer lifeboat *The Ruby and Arthur Reed* and a Sea King helicopter from the Air Sea Rescue Service to launch the annual Lifeboat Day in Cromer, 2 August 1984. This drill would be the last before Cromer's lifeboat was sent for a refit after serving the station for eighteen years. However, the refit would not be complete before the town received its new £430,000 Tyne Class lifeboat in early 1985.

View of the dig on Magdalen Street, Norwich, seen by visiting Norwich City Councillors on Wednesday 18 March 1987. The dig, which took place on council land, uncovered over 400 skeletons. These were all carefully removed by archaeologists and volunteers to make way for a new flats and shops complex on the site of this fourteenth- and fifteenth-century burial ground. Finds on the site included artefacts dating from the Iron Age and Bronze Age up to the medieval period. The area was the cemetery of the Church of St Margaret Incombusto, where many of the bodies of those hanged for their crimes at the nearby Maudly Gallows were buried.

Building Norwich Sports Village, 6 August 1987. Opened a few months later today the Sports Village is East Anglia's premier indoor tennis venue, has a fifty-five bedroom hotel, aqua park, restaurant and extensive conference, exhibition and sporting facilities.

The tenth Norwich Beer Festival, St Andrew's Hall, 30 October 1987. Beers of all descriptions and strengths from the four corners of Great Britain are showcased at this grand annual event. Supping from their beer festival glasses in the historic surroundings, drinkers are backed by live music as diverse as 'oompah' bands, to trad. jazz and even lunchtime recitals from St Andrew's own mighty organ. In 1987 Norfolk beers featured heavily in the awards. Reepham Brewery's Rapier, with its 'clean hoppy taste' was voted best special bitter. Woodforde's Wherry, which was the first ever brew when the brewery opened, won the best standard bitter award.

One of the most famous local images of modern times is that of the Eastern Counties double-decker bus which fell into an old chalk mine tunnel in Norwich. This opened up as the bus drove along Earlham Road on 3 March 1988. Tributes of praise were paid to the driver, Jimmy Pightling, who remained calm and helped passengers off to safety as the bus sank into the 30 ft deep cavern.

The first superloo in Norfolk was officially opened on Redwell Street in Norwich on Tuesday 27 September 1988. On its first week of operation the automatic toilet, which was supplied on six months' free trial, was used more than 200 times. The superloo gives each user fifteen minutes for 10p. After each use the walls and floors are washed and dried. Piped music is provided.

Scaffolding surrounded the South African war memorial near the Shirehall on Agricultural Hall Plain, Norwich, in mid-November 1988. The memorial, opened in November 1904 by Maj Gen A.S. Wynne, commemorates the 310 men from Norfolk who fell in the South African War 1899–1902. Cracked and stained, the old memorial needed urgent internal and external restoration. Disappearing from her pinnacle for a few months, the angel was fully repaired and returned to her rightful place by a specialist firm in Telford. The restoration cost £32,000.

The official opening ceremony of Norwich's new Crown Court, 25 November 1988. The Lord Chancellor, Lord Mackay of Clashfern (second right) has just unveiled the plaque, with Justice Moyland (left), Mr Justice Farquharson, presiding Judge of the South Eastern Circuit (second left) and Judge Blofield (right). The complex, built on the site of the Palace Gas Works, was built by Farrans Construction for £6½ million.

Fred Eva represents the feelings of all those who know the suffering of the Far Eastern prisoners of war during the Second World War at the memorial ceremony held as a protest against British representation at the funeral of Emperor Hirohito of Japan on 24 February 1989. Thirty thousand Europeans and Australians, 7,000 of them in the 18th (Eastern) Division from Norfolk, Suffolk and Cambridgeshire, were sent to fight for the island of Singapore in 1941. Within four months they were

either dead or taken into captivity at the Fall of Singapore in February 1942. Those who were imprisoned endured three years of totally inhumane degradation: they were sent as forced labour to work down mines or work with thousands of Malaysian coolies on the infamous railway of death through Thailand. Every sleeper along that railway equates to a life lost in its construction. Three whole battalions of brave Norfolk lads were sent to the debacle of Singapore. The feelings and sympathy for these men still run strong in the county, so it is not surprising that Fred was cheered as he spoke at the service. He said that the Duke of Edinburgh was attending the funeral for the establishment, not for ordinary people. Fred, who had served as a signaller in the 6th Battalion, Royal Norfolk Regiment had returned from the hell of captivity as a gaunt 7 stone skeleton, and sent his medals back to the Prime Minister, Margaret Thatcher, in a gesture of disgust.

The official launch of the Theatre Royal, Norwich, Development Appeal gets off to a resounding start at Black Friars Hall on 5 April 1989. The £2¾ million scheme was designed to take the theatre into the twenty-first century. This launch was well blessed, with £1 million pledged from city, county and district councils and £30,000 from a local charitable trust, augmented by cash gifts from major companies. The dignitaries are, left to right, Dick Condon, Theatre General Manager, Geoffrey Marshall, Theatre Royal Trust Chairman, Gerry McGurk, Appeal Chairman and Major Michael Roythorne, Appeal Director, and presenting the first £100,000 cheque is Mr John Alston, Chairman of Norfolk County Council.

Have you seen these men? Crimestoppers wish they hadn't. On 10 August 1988 two white policemen blacked up and donned curly wigs to re-enact an armed robbery on Aleks Szymanski's Jewellers on Castle Street, Norwich for Anglia TV's *Crimestoppers*. Their efforts brought laughs of derision from passers-by and a swipe from a Norwich City councillor, who said the men looked like 'overgrown Robinson's Gollywogs'. Disapproval was also voiced from the City Council's Equal Opportunities Committee Vice-Chair, Jackie Newman. Norfolk police said they had no black officers they could use. Anglia TV's press officer, Tom Walshe, commented that the reconstruction involved only a fleeting glimpse of the blackened men, and that they 'would regret very much if people took offence'.

East Anglia crafts have been undergoing something of a revival over the last ten years. David Baker of West Acre was one of a growing number of craftsmen reviving the ancient art of letter cutting. He is seen here working on a memorial for the late Sir Peter Roberts of Cockley Cley. His incisive skills have been honed over thirty years. Working mainly in Welsh slate, his favourite stone, his commissions include works for councils, churches, Ely Cathedral and even an AIDS hostel in London.

Celebrating twenty-five years of BBC Look East, 27 September 1989. Left to right: George Milner Smith, Programme Director, Kim Riley, Louise Priest and Stuart White. In a special feature memories were also shared by original producer Malcolm Freegard, who once had to step into the breech when filming at the Maddermarket theatre and dress up as an enormous caterpillar when the man who should have filled the costume did not turn up. Popular presenter Ian Masters, who fronted Look East between 1974 and 1983, shared a tale about a feature on St Bernard dogs, when the two dogs in the studio started fighting – and one bit him live on air.

It's so bracing! All along the east coast a strange and comparatively recent tradition dictates that certain folk may wish to brave the cold North Sea for a swim on Boxing Day, as seen here in 1989, or on New Year's Day.

In Norfolk we have a reputation for making things last, especially in the farming community, where machinery is expensive and is expected to be good value for money. In January 1990 brothers Gerald, Stanley and Donald Smith showed off what must be one of the supreme examples of farm vehicle endurance – their 1941 Allis Chalmers tractor, which was still in use on their farm at Forncett St Peter.

A carnival atmosphere always pervades Norwich as the streets become crammed with spectators to watch The Lord Mayor's Procession. Saturday 14 July 1990 was certainly no different. Here we see The Lingwood Cheerleaders with their pom-poms as they enter Upper King Street.

The Patterson family examine corn circles discovered at Gorleston Farm in July 1990. Found occasionally over the years in fields across Norfolk, in the early 1990s this strange phenomenon manifested itself in almost epidemic proportions. Some crop circles were blatant hoaxes while others were associated with strange lights and UFOs. Nobody was ever caught in the process of making one and although many theories were put forward there was no clear answer as to how they were actually created.

The cast of *Danton's Death*, with the guillotine they built to form the centrepiece of the play, November 1990. This theatrical performance was the first to be performed at the new city arts and music centre, The Waterfront, which opened in October 1990.

Procession of Witness and Expression of Private Devotion, Norwich, Good Friday 1991. More than 300 people of all denominations followed the cross through the city in the procession organised by the Norwich Council of Churches. Setting off from the cathedral they made their way via Hay Hill to St John's Roman Catholic Church for a short Service and then back to Hay Hill where the cross was erected, with members of the churches attending it until 4 pm.

The construction of the substructure of the Castle Mall, Norwich, during its completion phase in December 1991. The mall grew from these foundations to open as the city's showpiece shopping centre in 1993. Already containing a host of popular shops and the city's main post office and car parks, development of the complex continues with the soon to be completed multi-screen cinema.

The King's Morris Men hold aloft the May Garland and blow hard on their ox horns in the ancient tradition of warding off evil at King's Lynn, 1 May 1992. The morris men had braved the wind and rain earlier that morning to 'Dance Up' the Mayday Dawn at 5.15 am at Knightshill, the highest point in Lynn, to greet the sun.

The Theatre Royal, Norwich, faced an uncertain future after its closure in 1990 following lack of funding and a fire but as work progressed it rose anew with a growing team of backers. It was a great day when Sir Ian McKellen performed the topping out ceremony at the theatre on 28 May 1992.

Uncle and nephew retained Sheringham firemen Ian and Paul Richardson with their bravery certificates shortly after their presentation by Norfolk's Chief Fire Officer, Bryan Smith in January 1993. Sheringham fire brigade was called to Beeston Hill on 11 August 1992 to rescue two boys stuck in sand on the cliff side. In a difficult rescue Ian and Paul were winched down the cliffside to the boys to secure them with ropes before an RAF helicopter winched the whole group to safety.

Some of the characters from the King's Lynn pageant play *Siege* during rehearsals in the town centre on Monday 23 August 1993. Directed by Tom Crutchley with a cast of 250, the performance, sponsored by the *Eastern Daily Press*, commemorated the 350th Anniversary of the Siege of King's Lynn during the English Civil War. Also appearing were live horses, a 40 ft galleon, Norfolk Horn sheep from Anmer and Elly, and a Dexter cow from Swaffham with her calf.

On Sunday 14 November 1993 gales of storm force 10 gusting to 12 with a top speed of 83 knots and high seas lashed the North Norfolk coast. The Tayjack 1 jack-up platform broke free from its moorings just off West Runton and carried to Cromer. It ripped through the pier causing a 30 metre breach. Within days a programme for the pier's reconstruction was in hand. A rope suspension bridge was soon strung up across the gap so that lifeboat crews could cross to get to the lifeboat house at the end of the pier. Reconstruction began in January 1994 and on the 1 May it was reopened to the public by Rt Hon Mrs Gillian Shephard MP.

PC Bryan Edwards and Sgt Stephen Elliott-Hunter with the helicopter they will qualify in as Norfolk's first helicopter squad, February 1994. This was unveiled as the police's 'Eye in the Sky' to track and follow criminals from a height of 100 ft as they make their getaway and thus reduce the need for high speed car chases. The helicopter was initially flown by Stirling Helicopter pilots until Stephen and Bryan qualified to fly the forces' own aircraft.

Lord Mayor of Norwich Mr Roy Durrant with the 800-year-old City Charter granting self-government signed by Richard I in 1194 at the launch of Norwich 800 celebrations in May 1994. As part of a year of special events a Norwich 800 shop selling souvenirs and local books was set up in the Mall, the Castle was turned into an enormous birthday cake with candles among its turrets and a time capsule was buried at the foot of the steps of City Hall.

Children from Neatishead Primary School dance around the Maypole at Horning Staithe, 1 May 1994. In Norfolk the maypole is a wonderfully maintained tradition. Many schools still have poles both static and portable where the children, after a great deal of practice, peform this ancient rite at fetes and local festivities.

Prunella Scales with Norwich Playhouse Managing Director Henry Burke and Timothy West receive a cheque for £100,000 from the Foundation for Sport and the Arts at the Norwich Playhouse Gala held at the Theatre Royal in June 1994. The idea for the playhouse, to be situated at the city's disused Gun Wharf, was mooted in 1989 with the £2.5 million scheme for its construction launched in 1990. Building work commenced in 1992 and with generous donations from the Foundation for Sport and the Arts, Lottery funding of £400,000 and gifts from individuals, including many of our well-known actors and actreses, it opened in October 1995.

Fire crews attempt to quell the blaze at Norwich Central Library, 1 August 1994. The great black pall of smoke towered up above the city like a shroud ready to descend on the burnt remnants of our county's greatest literary repository. This affected not only the lending library but also the American Memorial Library and – for me, most horrific and irreplaceable loss of all – the Colman Rye Library of books and material of historical Norfolk interest, which was destroyed, along with most of the books from the Norfolk Studies Library. The losses caused by the fire are immeasurable but work goes on. Many local historians and researchers have done their best to reconstitute the

losses, members of the public responded wonderfully to the great book hunt and gradually the collection is building up again under the energetic and committed auspices of the local studies library staff. At the moment the library is divided between two separate locations but under a multi-million pound project a new central library built on the old site should open in 2001.

The well-respected and long remembered RSM Bert Fitt DCM, MSM (last RSM for the The Royal Norfolk Regiment) gives a final salute farewell as Britannia Barracks loses its last ties with the military on 16 December 1994. No last bugle call was sounded, no final retreat beaten for the barracks opened as the depot for The Norfolk Regiment in 1887. Cameron House, the last main occupied building which had acted as Regimental Museum, Regimental HQ for The Royal Anglian Regiment, The Royal Norfolk Regiment Association HQ and base for Norwich SSAFA closed. It was vacated and the museum was packed up and moved to its new base in the old Shirehall, while the other occupants moved to premises on the Aylsham Road TA Centre site.

Over 3,000 people, including many of the 900 workers from Nestlé, march down Chapel Field, Norwich, on Saturday 17 December 1994 to protest over the closure of the chocolate factory. The distinctive smell of chocolate production had been a familiar feature of the city since the factory founded by A.J. Caley began producing cocoa in the 1880s. The business was sold in 1918 to the African & Eastern Trading Company, who in turn sold it to John Mackintosh & Sons in 1932. Rowntree Mackintosh held the company for many years until the early 1990s, when they were bought out by Swiss chocolate giants Nestlé. In December 1994 Nestlé announced a £15 million cost-cutting exercise and closed the factory with the loss of 900 jobs.

Fire crews attempt to quell the fire which burnt out the Assembly House, Norwich, 12 April 1995. Pictures, paintings and period decorations were severely smoke damaged or totally destroyed in the blaze, which closed one of the city's most popular social and cultural venues for months, while it was restored in a £384,000 project.

The dissatisfaction of Norwich City FC fans with the Chairman Robert Chase was clearly expressed at their match with Nottingham Forest on 12 April 1995. Before the match a special bank of speakers was brought in to relay positive and upbeat music to the capacity crowd. Mr Chase said: 'We want to liven things up a little; this is a crucially important game for us.' But it could also be argued that the music was some attempt to drown out the angry chants of city fans inside and outside the ground. Ten thousand red cards were distributed by anti-Chase demonstrators, and were held up at half and full time. Boycotts were threatened for the new season when City were relegated, and continued until Mr Chase left. He resigned at the end of the following season, and has been replaced by television cooking personality Delia Smith.

Closed circuit television cameras observing the streets of Norwich were officially switched on on Tuesday 25 July 1995. Seen here is the nerve centre of the cameras at St Andrew's multi-storey car park on Duke Street. Fifteen cameras were installed, covering the city's main shopping streets, Magdalen Street and Rose Lane. The £650,000 project was funded jointly by the City and County Councils, with contributions from businesses and a Home Office grant.

One of the opening scenes of *Fire From Heaven*. Bishop Godwin (played by Theatre Royal Chief Executive Peter Wilson) argues with the Prior of Lewes and Prior Turbe over what should be done with the body of St William of Norwich. The production, celebrating the 900th anniversary of the founding of Norwich Cathedral was narrated by Donal Sinden. Performed in the cathedral cloisters, the play featured incidents from the history of Norwich Cathedral including the Tombland fair riot, invasion by the Commonwealth iconoclasts, fire in the organ and the visit of King George VI.

The view across the marshes at Salthouse, 21 February 1996. Over the previous forty-eight hours the eastern counties had been subject to severe snowstorms and high seas. Roads became clogged with snow drifts, abandoned cars and jackknifed lorries. The sea broke the shingle bank defences at Salthouse, pouring across the marshes and reduced the village green to a mire. In the worst storms to hit the village since 1953, the coast road was under 4 ft of water and waves lapped at the doors of the village pub and post office. Although the bank was breached it reduced the flow, and luckily this time no homes were flooded out.

Norwich Town Crier David Bullock and City Whiffler James 'Bert' Brenner (right) share a joke about Whiffler's privileges after the Lord Mayor's Procession, Norwich, 14 July 1996.

Traditional marshman Eric Edwards at work stacking the harvested reed on the River Ant at How Hill, January 1997.

Angry parents and children voice their protest at the closure of St Augustine's Swimming Pool, January 1997. The council-owned and run pool was closed on the eve of a major swimming competition in December 1996 when structural faults were found in the building. In March 1997 the pool's fate was sealed at a closed meeting of the city's ruling Labour group, where it was decided that the cost of repairs was too great and that it should remain closed. No further pool was proposed for the site, and demolition began in September 1997.

Stephen Fisher puts apples through his 1850 apple scratter at Wroxham Barns, March 1997. When over 200 years of cider making tradition came to an end with the closure of Gaymer's Cider Works in Attleborough in 1994 redundant employee Stephen Fisher decided that he would begin his own, unique, cider making business. Beginning very much as the founder of Gaymer's would have done, Stephen uses local apples, old presses and traditional methods. His delicious Kingfisher Farm cider and apple juice is now enjoyed all over the county. It is a delight to see Stephen take his presses to demonstrate this ancient skill at various country shows and fairs across Norfolk – and of course to sample the product!

Joint support for Compassion in World Farming is given by Norwich political candidates at the CIFW stand on Hay Hill, Norwich, 24 April 1997. They are, from the left, Norwich South candidates Andrew Aalders-Dunthorne (Liberal), Charles Clarke (Labour) and Adrian Holmes (Green), with Norwich North candidates Paul Young (Liberal) and Dr Ian Gibson (Labour). I wonder what we will make of 'mad cow disease' and beef restrictions when we look back on the 1990s.

National Lottery grants brought joy to a number of Norfolk-based projects on 30 July 1997. Ilkooshar Malarta from Norwich Puppet Theatre is all smiles about the organisation's £4,886 grant. Other Norfolk groups to benefit from the £113,223 handout included the Norwich City Concert Band, Hillside Avenue School, Friends of the Sainsbury Centre and Bowthorpe Clapperboard Theatre.

Strangers' Hall Museum, an ancient merchant's house with period room layouts and a wonderful collection of toys and costumes. Its displays enchanted generations, but because the old building does not comply with modern fire regulations it was forced to close in November 1998. Plans are afoot for the Friends of Stranger's Hall to take on the task of raising the £150,000 capital to enable the museum to undergo the necessary modifications for it to open again.

A ring of sand bags surrounds the Bronze Age timber circle dubbed 'Sea' or 'Wood' Henge at Holme-next-the-Sea. In 1998 field work was begun by the Norfolk Archaeological Unit on the recently exposed ring. In January 1999 a national newspaper put the site on its cover and massive public interest ensued as hundreds visited it. As spring passed into late summer the interest did not abate as the eliptical ring of fifity-five close-set oak timbers, dated to about 2000BC, had to be moved to be preserved at the specialist centre on Flag Fen. A number of protests were lodged against this by interested parties including druids. The circle has now been removed and the village of Holme may return to peace again. Now the real work begins in researching who the people were that built it – and why they did so.

Robert Kett and his men raise the standard and march down Wymondham Market Place on their way to confront Lord Sheffield on the Abbey Meadow, Saturday 10 July 1999. This recreation was all part of Kett '99 a celebration held in the town on 9, 10 and 11 July to mark the 450th anniversary of Kett's Rebellion in July 1549. The rebellion had begun at the town fair in protest at injustice in the county, particularly objecting to enclosures, and was led by local tanner Robert Kett and his brother William. They marched on Norwich and two armies were sent to quash the rebellion which was finally beaten at Dussindale where 3,000 of Kett's followers were killed. After 2 years of planning, this happier event in 1999 had not only re-enactments, the unveiling of a commemorative plaque, plays and special concerts but also brought together the largest ever reunion of the Kett family from all over the world.

In 1999 The Most Venerable Order of St John of Jerusalem celebrated its nonacentenary. Its most high profile arm is the St John Ambulance. Order services were held across the country to mark this special anniversary. Here are the officiating clergy and assembled dignitaries for the Nonacentenary Enrolment Service for Badgers and Cadets at the Priory Church of St Peter and St Paul, Carbrooke, on Sunday 17 October 1999. They are, left to right: Revd Sue Foster, County Lay Chaplain Mike Skinner, Georgina Holloway Area President, Brig W.E.I. Forsythe-Yorke OBE County Commander, Col C.E. Knight MBE Knight of the Order, County Chaplain Hugh Edgell, Mrs Scott Superintendent in Chief and Dame of the Order, and Lynford Brunt County Commissioner, Norfolk St John Ambulance.

Acknowledgements

I wish to extend my personal thanks to the following who have so generously contributed images and information to make this book possible: Basil Gowan, Philip Standley, Paul Standley, Dick Middleton, Rhoda Bunn, Captain Philip Watson of the 9th/12th Royal Lancers (Prince of Wales's), Jane Scarf of Abacus Video, Andy Hutcheson from Norfolk Archaeological Unit, Nick Walmsley, Editor of *Dirigible*, all the staff at Norwich City Library's Norfolk Studies Library whose commitment, helpfulness and knowledge of their collection is a credit to their profession. I also wish to record heartfelt thanks to David Clayton, Andy Archer, Maggie Secker and all the listeners of BBC Radio Norfolk; especially those who have so kindly shared their memories with me.

Over my years of writing, the characters and stories around me have never ceased to amaze me; I wish to thank all those, too numerous to mention, who have so kindly helped me by donating or loaning images or providing information for my research. I have attempted to obtain permission from all copyright holders of the photographs used herein. If there are any omissions in my acknowledgements please forgive me; no breach of those rights was intended.

The last thirty years and the significant images of those times in this county have been best recorded by the photographers of the Eastern Daily Press. Consequently, it is a very big thank you that I extend to Dennis Whitehead and the staff of the Eastern Counties Newspapers Library who have enabled me to use in this book the poignant images of our more modern history from their collection.

Special thanks are due, as ever, to Terry Burchell for his photographic wonders. Finally, but by no means least, I would like to thank my family for their on-going support and encouragement, especially by darling wife Sarah for her additional research work and love for this temperamental author.

Mr Bales playing Old Father Time at Wymondham, *c.* 1911.